Wisdom Rising:

a self-help guide to personal transformation,
spirituality, and mind/body/spirit holistic living

by
Vaishāli

©2008 Purple Haze Press®

Publisher: Vaishāli and Purple Haze Press®

Purple Haze Press Chief Editor: Pela Tomasello

Cover design and illustrations by: Brian Narelle

Special Thanks to: Aime and Steve McCrory, Brian and Robin Narelle, Maxine Chavez, Joe and Janet Cosgrove, Randy Peyser, Pela Tomasello, Sarah Bartholomew, Jeff Bedrick, and Allen Jay Friedman

© 2008 Vaishāli and Purple Haze Press®

Purple Haze Press books can be ordered through booksellers or by visiting www.PurpleHazePress.com or www.PurpleV.com or by contacting:

Purple Haze Press
2430 Vanberbilt Beach Road, 108
PMB 167
Naples, FL 34109

First Printing, July 2008

Library of Congress Control Number 2008922982

Other books by Vaishāli, "You Are What You Love®" and the "You Are What You Love, Play book"

ISBN 978-0-9773200-6-6

1. New Age   2. Love   3. Self-Help   4. Spirituality
5. Consciousness Education

Wisdom Rising:

a self-help guide to personal transformation,
spirituality, and mind/body/spirit holistic living

*Dedicated to my Dad,
my first Spiritual Teacher.*

Table of Contents

Section 3   *Spirituality*

Section 4   *Mind/Body/Spirit*

Foreword

I have found over years of doing speaking engagements, individual sessions and call-in radio shows that there are some concepts that people cannot hear enough times. One of these is the Spiritual Law that *we do not have love, we are love*. There are Universal Truths like this that you, the reader, will see over and over again in this book.

The repeated reinforcement of these profound Truths is neither there by accident nor a redundancy that simply escaped proper editing. It is there as a visual psycho-spiritual healing. Human beings have a talent of incessantly and tenaciously fixating on a constant drone of negative "inner dialog" messages about their value, power and worth. The purpose behind these echoed ideas is to make the Truth about our Divinity as clear, certain, familiar and tangible as we have made our fears and insecurities.

I feel it is also worth mentioning that I wrote this book for all the people who told me that they wanted a book with short, quick chapters, as they tended to consume a book slowly over time. They wanted a book that they not only could learn a lot from, but also would allow them to read a few chapters, then come back to it in a week or month and be able to pick it up, without having to remember precisely the focus of the earlier segments.

Each chapter is short and sweet and stands alone. The entire book covers different aspects of wisdom, so it is not slighting the reader in quality of content or depth of practical knowledge.

My favorite joke about my life is that before I was born, God asked, "Who wants to learn from more pain?" I must have thought he said "more gain" and asked for extra.

My life challenges began at birth. I was born with a birth defect on my face. Although I underwent several cosmetic surgeries to correct the problem, it was still visually evident until in my late teens, early twenties. My parents divorced and remarried numerous times. Often this revolving door of parents brought with it the dynamics of alcoholism, abuse and years of parental neglect.

At the age of eight, I could barely read or write. I did not even know how to spell my last name! As a result I was placed in a special education program designed to bring problem students up to speed with the rest of their class. Over the next few years my special education teacher patiently spent hour after hour teaching me how to read, write and speak properly. She became the nurturing, unconditionally loving mother figure I so desperately needed. Then suddenly, she was violently murdered by someone who wanted to make the crime look like it was a ritualistic killing. Needless to say her homicide was inconceivably horrible. I was so traumatized by her death, I suppressed all memories of her until a few years later when the police caught the assumed killer. With the resurgence of the incident in everyone's conversations, I allowed my memory of her to resurface.

Like most everyone else, I have been lied to and cheated on by nearly all my intimate relationships. I also went through an ugly divorce, what has become a normal right of passage into adulthood.

I have been diagnosed terminal twice: once from an illness and the second time from car accident injuries. I have experienced years and years of the kind of physical pain you would jump off a building to get out of. (Good thing I lived on the first floor most of this time.) When it came time for the car accident trial, I lost. I was buried in legal and medical expenses. I lost my business and my entire life savings. If suffering were a buffet, I have apparently sampled everything at least once and gone back for seconds on the really juicy items.

The gift of earning a Ph.D. in suffering is that I learned how to resolve it and use it for my benefit. I clearly recognize what causes this limitation we call suffering in the flow of our lives. I also understand what wisdom releases it, or at the very least, diminishes its destructive impact. To have any authentic value in life, wisdom has to be practical in both its understanding as well as its application. If the wisdom you have is not pulling your butt consistently out of life's many fires, it is meaningless! Real wisdom detoxifies you and develops within you the strength, power and agility to handle whatever obstacles life throws your way.

The process of repeated self-resurrection has blessed me with a profound canon of wisdom that covers vast territory in the realm of the human experience. Every life challenge that is a source of suffering is like an oyster stimulated by a grain of sand, resulting in the growth of a pearl. In my case suffering produced great pearls of wisdom. Wisdom Rising is a collection of those pearls, strung together to create a jeweled accessory stylish enough to adorn and compliment the remarkable and extraordinary wardrobe know as the human experience.

Wear it with all my love and Blessings, and dazzle the world with your stellar, eternal, Divine beauty.

Love, Vaishāli
April 2008

A Personal Introduction to Emanuel Swedenborg

I'd like to take this opportunity to introduce to you, formally and most lovingly, an exceptional man it has been my deepest honor to refer to as "my boyfriend". He is not your typical boyfriend. He is in the Guinness Book Of World Records for having one of the world's highest IQ's. Stanford University voted him one of the most brilliant people to have ever lived. Already you can see we are not talking about your average "boyfriend" résumé. Oh, and one more thing he currently does not have a physical body; he died in 1772. I stole the title of my first book *You Are What You Love* directly from his writings. As you can see, I only steal from the best.

My "boyfriend" is Emanuel Swedenborg. He was born in Stockholm, Sweden in 1688. A bit before my time, but true love does not recognize age or geographic differences. Swedenborg began his life mastering every known science. He studied with Sir Isaac Newton and Sir Edmund Haley. When he heard about microbes, he ground his own glass and made his own microscope. When he heard about Galileo, he ground his own glass and made his own telescope. He was a metallurgist and invented many mining safety techniques. He constructed the first working hang glider, long before the Wright brothers. It is on display in the Smithsonian Institute. He drew up a working blueprint for a submarine. He wrote over 150 scientific works. He discovered the purpose of the cerebellum and wrote 4 volumes on the human brain, complete with the most advanced drawings of his time. He determined the relationship between respiration and the nervous system, and between respiration and the movement of cerebral spinal fluid. He deciphered the function of the pituitary gland, and the body's endocrine system. He has oftentimes been called the Swedish Da Vinci. And in his spare time he was also a member of Sweden's parliament. I could spend the rest of this book filling it with details about his many, many achievements . . . but I think you get the idea.

What impressed me the most about Swedenborg was not what he did, but *why* he did it. Swedenborg felt that his scientific explorations were meant to assist him in a "bigger picture" quest. Swedenborg said that what he really wanted to determine was where the Soul resided in the human experience. All his scientific accomplishments were simply the means he was using to understand and investigate that larger truth Gestalt.

Swedenborg had been able to control his breath and enter into a trance-like state of concentrated focus since he was a small child. In retrospect, it is speculated that by sustaining an intense concentrated state of focus for prolonged periods of time, he was able to accomplish his many dazzlingly brilliant scientific discoveries. At the age of 56, after a lifetime of practicing this concentrated focus technique, Swedenborg said the veil between the physical and the Spiritual worlds dissolved, and he was able to see and hear the Spiritual realms with the same detail and clarity of the physical world. Every day for the remainder of his life, about another 28 years, Swedenborg spoke with Angels and Spiritual beings that dwelt in higher and lower order realms.

The list of people who have been highly influenced by Sweden-borg is as long and impressive as Swedenborg's scientific creden-tials. The great German philosopher Immanuel Kant, American existentialist Ralph Waldo Emerson, Benjamin Franklin, Thomas Jefferson, Helen Keller, artist William Blake, the great Zen Bud-dhist teacher D. T. Suzuki, archetype and dream work pioneer Carl Jung, poet Walt Whitman, Andrew Carnegie and writer Stephen King are only a few. My boyfriend has influenced the people we most credit with molding Western civilization; yet most people today have never heard of him. It seems a crisis of consciousness that people know more about their favorite sitcom actor or actress than they do about Emanuel Swedenborg!

Like the great sleeping prophet Edgar Cayce, Swedenborg was able to ask questions and get remarkably wise and prophetic information from non-physically based sources. However, un-like Cayce, Swedenborg remembered everything in great detail and did not lose consciousness while communicating with the other side. He could have a lucid and intimate conversation with a group of Angels at the same time he was enjoying tea with friends or attending a parliament meeting.

There are many documented accounts of Swedenborg commu-nicating with the "other side" and then extending that infor-mation to those around him. These stories have since become known as Swedenborg's "minor miracles". Swedenborg himself never actually wrote about any of them. He felt they were not very important and did not want people to get distracted from the understanding of how we relate to Spiritual realities, which is the main thrust of all his writings.

Personally, I find Swedenborg's minor miracles fascinating, because they validate so exquisitely the authentic quality of his written wisdom. There are numerous stories of people who contacted Swedenborg because loved ones had died with sensitive information they took to their graves. When the survivors needed that information, they would ask Swedenborg to talk with the deceased friends or family on the "other side" and get what was needed. Swedenborg even provided that service for the Queen of Sweden, who afterwards became extremely loyal and dedicated to him. There are at least two accounts of Swedenborg letting people know of a fire that was happening some distance away and providing details of this event as it happened. Remember that Swedenborg lived in the 18th century, long before the telegraph, telephone, television or any form of mass communication. For Swedenborg to provide consistently accurate information involving situations known only by a deceased person, for him to reliably share in real-time, information about events, hundreds of miles away, is a pretty mean trick if you are just making it up. Swedenborg was even asked who would be the next person in the room with them that was going to die. He not only got the date and time right, but the clock by the man's bedside stopped at the exact moment of death! Swedenborg knew the date and exact time not only of other people's deaths, but also of his own. When asked how he knew these things, Swedenborg always had the same answer. . . . the Angels told him.

Swedenborg said it was revealed to him that the entire purpose of his earlier scientific career was to prepare him for his later work as a mystic. Swedenborg wrote over 35 volumes of work on the nature of the Spiritual world, and how what we do in the physical world affects where we live Spiritually. He wrote over three and half million words on how the Spiritual realms are organized. And don't forget this is without the benefit of word processing, spell check, or Google. I can see why such a strict scientific discipline was involved in the pre-training of Swedenborg's perspective. If it turned out that creating a GPS of the Spiritual realm was *my* J-O-B, I would be a bit biased. I would start out by describing what the Angels were wearing, who had the most colorful aura and what jokes were circulating in what level of Heaven . . . clearly hell would not have any jokes, because that would be too much fun. Swedenborg was not distracted by the typical way we observe reality. He was trained in nothing but the facts, long before Dragnet. Swedenborg brought us a timeless and incorruptible view of ultimate reality.

Swedenborg's definition of Heaven and hell is also very straightforward. Heaven is a place or state of being that is unlimited in nature. Hell is a place or state of being that is limited. Swedenborg pointed out that no one needs to die to experience these states; they are available to us right here on the Earth. Although what we experience here is not the real Heaven and hell - those are non-physical states of existence.

Furthermore Swedenborg said that the reason the Earth exists is to provide us with an advanced education in the Spiritual Law: *you are what you love, and you love whatever you are giving your attention to.* Here on the Earth plane it is an unavoidable reality that we must feel the direct result of what we give our attention to. If you spend your time worrying, you most likely have already noticed it is a rather hellish quality of life. Swedenborg and this Spiritual Law will be referenced many times during the course of this book. Rather than laboriously repeating who Swedenborg is and why this Law is essential in understanding the meaning and purpose of created life, I felt this one introduction should be sufficient in carrying us through the remaining chapters.

After finishing this book, I have no doubt that you too will want to refer to Swedenborg as a "friend". Feel free. After all, you have been formally introduced, and there is always plenty of love to go around. Since Swedenborg is a pristine member of Heaven's community, he naturally has an unlimited number of "friends." Just remember to pass on my love the next time you run into him.

Section 1 ~ Self Help

Lucid Dreaming

I have been doing dream work for as long as I can remember. As a child, dream reality seemed to supersede what we laughingly call "waking reality". Like most people who commit to dream work, I had achieved a very casual, superficial level of lucid dreaming. Lucid dreaming is a state of consciousness where the dreamers are fully aware that they are asleep, and that what they are experiencing is a state of reality completely manufactured by the dreaming mind. Just about everyone has experienced a flash of lucid recognition during a dream - knowing that they are in fact "just dreaming". However, lucid dreaming as I am defining it here is a more intensified and sustained state of dream realization. At its best, lucid dreaming is a completely conscious state of mind where the doors to the conscious and unconscious minds are fully open to each other - available for exploration, examination and to be fearlessly embraced.

Imagine the value in being able to ask a dream character or image: *Who are you? Who am I? What can I do for you? What would you like to tell me? What do you feel I should know?* Imagine the dream interpretation problems that could be solved by going immediately to the dream character and getting the skinny directly from the source. Imagine the possibility of rapidly accelerating the amount of growth done in a single evening's nocturnal journeys. Imagine the benefits to be had when the dream state you experience is fully "awake" to the reality that *this* is what you are trying to tell yourself; *this* is what is going on behind the closed doors of your own mind. Once lucid, what was previously the circuitous road of non-lucid dreaming could now be traveled instantly, directly and most importantly clear to question and answer discourse. It is like the know thyself quest gone completely, psychedelically accessible in a Kurt Vonnegut sort of way!

As a hardcore dream worker, I'd read about experiments at the Lucidity Institute by Dr. Stephen LaBerge on the *DreamLight* before this device hit the streets - or the sheets as it were. The *DreamLight is* a creation designed to augment the dreamer's state of awareness from the typical R.E.M. into the hyperspace state of dream lucidity. The dreamer wears a mask that flashes when R.E.M. is achieved to signal to the dreamer that he is experiencing a dream-produced reality. Imagine my surprise when my pal, Howard Rheingold, the then editor of *The Whole Earth Review* and co-author of *Exploring The World Of Lucid Dreaming* with Stephen LaBerge, Ph.D., asked me if I was interested in helping the Lucidity Institute refine the *DreamLight*. "Am I interested?" I asked Howard, flabbergasted, "Of course I'm interested! I would walk naked down Market Street in downtown San Francisco for the chance to try the *DreamLight!!*" Howard was hardly impressed. From his perspective I would have walked naked down Market Street just for the hell of it. So Howard, completely unfettered by my vocal dramatics, told me that Dr. LaBerge was soliciting the assistance of established lucid dreamers to support the Lucidity Institute in the final phases of completion of the *DreamLight*. This marked the beginning of my relationship with the Lucidity Institute.

All the people I met who were associated with the Lucidity Institute were like a dream come true themselves. They were all very generous with their time, open hearted, caring, lovely people. Doing dream work in groups can provide amazing support and insight. Everyone at the Lucidity Institute was motivated by the need to direct their attention to self-growth and self-mastery. I learned so much from those group sessions and sharing: everything from technical tricks of the trade, to how to recognize and overcome personal limitations. The first thing that I learned from my work in the lucid dream realm was how uncooperative my own mind was with itself. I was shocked and astonished to discover how uninterested my lucid dream characters were in responding to my questions or in helping on any level. Could I really be a house that deeply divided against itself? Could the major activity of the unconscious/unintegraded aspects of mind really be giving each other the bird? When working with other lucid dream workers, I found that they too had not made their minds their friends. In fact, one of the first things that people who start this conscious interaction with their dream characters report is that the dream characters either ignored the presence of the dreaming personality, or were not forthcoming in providing information when asked.

There are two pieces of advice that I got from Dr. LaBerge that I will never forget. The first is that dream characters will never tell you what you expect. This completely makes sense; after all, the other dream characters are fragments of our own mind that we are experiencing as separate. That is why they are appearing as "separate" from ourselves. The second bit of advice was the old Christian adage to "love thy neighbors." I still remember the forcefulness of Dr. LaBerge's face and voice when he leaned over to reinforce the power of this approach. "It works in your dreams! Love everyone you see in your dreams. Just like the old Christian adage 'Love thy neighbors'. *It really works in your dreams."*

That was the piece I needed! I needed to unconditionally love

myself in order to make my mind my friend. The lack of coop-
eration absolutely coincided with the absence of unconditional
love these various parts of mind suffered from. I have spent years
following that advice and speaking and acting in an unconditionally loving manner in my lucid dreams. I have focused on
remembering that what I am looking at is my own mind. The
message I most want communicated to it is that it is *one with
unconditional love and acceptance*. The results have been phenomenal! I have gone from disengaged, disinterested dream characters to dream characters that come and teach me new things.
Dream characters even come to me when I am in a non-lucid
state, make me look them directly in the eye, and remind me,
"We met here last night . . . remember? We met here last night."
Until I finally do remember that I met them in a dream, and
they are showing up now to assist me in waking up!

Whenever other lucid dreamers come to me and share their
disappointment in their lucid encounters, I always try to un-
derscore that what they are looking at is their own lack of unconditional love and acceptance within themselves. It is merely
showing up in their lucid dreams, because this is an arena we
cannot fake it in. We are either unified, or we are not; we either
love, accept and cooperate with ourselves, or we do not. The first
step is to *honestly* see where we are in relationship to embracing ourselves with love and tolerance, versus how much of our
interior have we fragmented and divided with criticism, doubt,
impatience and fear. Prior to my lucid dreaming, if someone had
come to me and told me that I was not making my mind my
friend, I would not have believed it. I would have assumed that
they had mistaken me for someone else or were on some kind of
perceptually distorting pharmaceutical. I had to experience it for
myself. I had to run straight up against my own inner resistance

to personal wholeness before I was willing to admit there was a problem. "We have seen the enemy and it is us." And to think, all this time I'd been "Sleeping With the Enemy."

Lucid dreams are an incredible experience. They are very, very vibrant, amazingly alive with brilliant color. There is a sense of seeing with enhanced dimensional clarity. What I have most enjoyed about lucid dreaming, aside from the advantages of these immediate self-love healing sessions, is the opportunity to have a realm in which I can practice showing up utterly fearless. I know I am dreaming. I know I have an immortal dream body that cannot be harmed, injured or killed. Therefore, I can literally face my greatest inner demons and transform them into loving Angels. In many lucid dreams I have made a request, such as " to encounter a part of my mind that has a gift for me." I can then take off flying and allow that moment of meeting to come to me. I have learned not to force life from my lucid dreams, but rather to surrender into unconditional trust. I know and trust that I will be there for myself, guiding myself when and where I most need it.

The insight I have gained on how my mind works and what the different parts of it look like, is simply astounding and life altering. I remember once in a lucid dream coming across a dream character that was a two-faced, disembodied head that lived in a box. When I asked my personal "Jack in the Box" who he was, the answer that came back was perfect. The two-faced head introduced itself as "the ego"! Of course! A part of the mind that is thoroughly disconnected from the wisdom of the heart, that is deceitful, that resides in an altogether limiting place. I remember how hard I laughed; how flawless this imagery was; how sobering its effects are whenever I take myself too seriously. And, no, I didn't get the large fries!

There are no limits to where one can go in a lucid dream. Well, none that I have found yet. It costs nothing but awareness on the part of the dreamer. The feeling of invincible wholeness I have upon awaking from a lucid dream is the greatest drug of choice I have ever found. For me, lucid dreaming has solidified the Eastern concept that we are all dreaming this waking reality level of existence. Lucid dreaming is the last thing I devote my attention to when falling asleep at night and the first thing I celebrate upon "awakening" in the morning. I could not encourage people enough to attempt this state of focused attention. I have neither found a downside to lucid dreaming, nor have I come close to exhausting its potential. I always try to include lucid dreaming in all the Spiritual teachings and writings that I do, because if there was a faster, better way to grow, love and liberate oneself, I'd be doing it.

The Voodoo's and Don'ts of American Culture

*P*ost-modern American culture is not famous for embracing Spiritual values. And you thought that outer space is the only thing that operates in a vacuum. Welcome to our world — a high-tech spiritual wasteland. If it cannot be measured, weighed, separated in a particle accelerator, or grown in a Petrie dish, most people in the Western world are going to have a problem with its credibility. After all, if you can't stick a pin in it, slap a Latin label on it, or point to it on the Periodic Table of Elements, then it does not really exist . . . right?

Whatever the Spiritual traditional practice is, it most likely exists for one inspired purpose: to move us out of our limited, cerebral method of thinking and relating to life, into the unlimited wisdom and knowingness of our Hearts. And that is truly not just the final frontier, but also the longest and greatest journey we will ever make. But to start that trip, most people in North America have to be dragged, kicking and screaming. Or, they insist on doing it with a death grip on their scientific journals, data, and research materials. Spiritual traditional practices are designed to activate something higher, greater, more comprehensive in the human experience than just the simple secretions of the frontal lobe. Think not? How many people do you know would be insulted by the suggestion that their intellectual opinions are *not* the most important and profound things in the Universe? I rest my case.

Is this really the enlightened age? You would never know it by looking at mainstream America, which is more a Spiritual tradition stepchild of the modern world. The only established traditions we have in this culture were brought here from somewhere else and not even generally accepted by the rest of us. Thank God it is not up to the FDA, TSA, FBI, KmyA, Customs or any other government regulated agency to determine the legality or value of a practice. If we had to wait for the AMA to determine the healing benefits of meditation, we would be taking a little yellow gel-cap to quiet our minds or watch the breath.

I have great respect for traditions that allow us to bypass the ego-created self and connect to our Spiritual Identity. That action is deeply, and in most cases, fundamentally needed and healthy. That is the purpose and value behind, within and around these practices. It is the culturally brave Soul that resists the ethnocentric conditioned social current to acknowledge only what science deems useful and precious — to reach beyond to what cannot be seen, into the Infinite, exploring the archetypical mysteries that lay beyond the corporeal.

Imagine an America where the cost of seeing your local shaman at a drumming circle was included in your health insurance plan. Or a tax revenue system where the price of smudge sticks, rattles and Holy ash was a tax deduction line on your 1040 form. Picture a mainstream USA, where parents have their child's astrology chart drawn up before they go in for their first round of immunization shots. Visualize walking into your doctor's office and seeing a "localized field of energy" and "auric chart" right next to the anatomy poster. Or having a computer with spell-check that can even recognize "auric" as a word! And wouldn't it be nice if we not only had an eye doctor, but also an "I" doctor.

Consider what America would be like if we, like the Tibetans, practiced preparing for death on a daily basis. The Tibetan culture embraces death as an upgrade into a greater reality, which allows for a much less traumatizing response to that 100% probability that someone in your life will die someday. Traditionally training the mind that death is a natural part of life, and reminding ourselves of this reality in the flow of our everyday life, really does take the sting out of the whole mortality thing. Especially for that ever predictable moment when we finally realize that our lives here are finite. It seems pretty obvious that there are some very healthy and empowering side effects to a ritualized practice of accepting an ultimately irrevocable and eventually universal ubiquitous death process. Not to mention that our HMO would be ecstatic that we'd pull the plug instead of keeping a loved one alive in an unconscious state for years on life support.

So, for those of us who are willing to avail ourselves to the counter-culture movement of an integrated Spiritual practice of some kind, any kind, we will have to be happy with the benefits and grounding influences that tradition brings us. For in this country, it is unlikely that the popular obsession with empirical, double-blind, better living through chemistry, Underwriters Laboratory tested, government inspected, grade "A" ways of embracing reality will be fading away anytime soon. Most people prefer working from the outside inwards. We, as a group, are much fonder of caustically telling each other "you have a brain - use it!" than valuing and taking advantage of time honored methods of accessing wisdom and balancing one's life from the inside out.

To all those out there ready and willing to blaze your own Spiritual traditional trail, for everyone strong enough to swim against the cultural tide of intellectualism, for those of you amongst us with stronger hearts than know-it-all egos, many Divine Blessings to you. May you find what no atomic powered microscope can see. May you explore inner space and go deeper than Dr. Timothy Leary on an acid trip. May your underdog methods of discerning what is useful and wise always serve and strengthen you. May you continue to challenge those around you, who myopically limit reality to only what their five senses can comprehend and acknowledge. But most importantly of all, may these creative and imaginative means of engaging with life and the mysteries it contains make you a more loving, compassionate, sensitive and insightful being. Or as the ancient runes and I Ching tell us: Rock on, babies!

Creativity:
The Favorite Drug of Choice

*T*hroughout time all human beings have one thing in common. We love being creative; we live for it. When your day or week was a struggle to get through, how many times did the mere expectation of a creative venture get you through the grind? Maybe you were looking forward to playing music with your friends, or going to dance class. Perhaps your drug of choice is a round of golf, or working on your classic car to cherry that baby out. There is nothing more life affirming than creativity itself. An added bonus is that creativity comes naturally to every person. We are all born knowing how to play. Creating toy horses from brooms or mops is a ubiquitous childhood experience.

So, why the collective addiction to creativity? The answer is very simple. Creating is what God creatures do. After all God's nickname is "The Creator." Prime Source kicked it all off by creating the Heavens and the Earth. And Prime Source created this Earthly/Heavenly something, out of a pure void, from absolute nothingness. It is in our Spiritual DNA to create. We all strongly desire that 0 to 60 creative rush. Without creativity we would not be able to reach enlightenment, which is creating Self-realization from ignorance. Once again we mimic the big "G" in manifesting "something" from "nothing." Creativity is how we end our suffering. We all have the God given creative intelligence to create a new response to any and all limitations. Do not get me wrong. Some of us have made an art form out of re-creating our stories and limiting issues ad nauseum. However, as God creatures having a human experience, the potential to create an ending to the source of all unhappiness is our birthright.

There are two elements to creativity that take us from amateur creators on a hobby level, to master creators of our own Self-actualized destiny. Those key elements are imagination and practice. Ask any inventor what is the first step to any creative project, and he will tell you that first he had to imagine the outcome he wanted before directing the flow of creative juices. Creating enlightenment is no different. You have to be able to imagine that you are capable of liberating your mind, or you will not realize that you can. You have to be able to imagine that you are one with Divine Love and Wisdom before you can create an alignment with your Divinity, value, power and worth, that no one and no thing on this planet has the power to change or diminish. You have to be able to imagine that all life is interconnected and equally God and Holy before you can create the perception of Universal Divine Oneness. You have to be able to imagine your true nature as infinite and unlimited before you can create the embodiment of that reality. Creativity has no substance or direction without imagination.

The powers of Creativity improve with the element of practice. Consider the first time you made a model airplane, took a piano or tennis lesson, made a chocolate soufflé, or painted a picture. Your first exposure to that creative task was most likely not your finest hour with that medium. Mastery is inseparable from practice. It is like "How do you get to Carnegie Hall?" Practice! Practice! Without practice we have no way of developing and building those creative muscles. Without practice we do not have the means to develop the skill of creating a new response to old problems. Without practice at growing beyond limitation, we do not have the power or the ability to do so. Anytime we are not practicing ending our suffering, we are practicing recreating and extending our suffering. And most likely, that is not what any-one would consciously choose to empower with their creative time here on Earth.

With practice also comes self-confidence and self-assurance. When you look at your life, what practice do you see emerging? Is your practiced habit revealing an established healthy confi-dence in relating to yourself as a force of Divine Love, no matter what life throws at you? Or do you see a pattern of "confidence" that you will not have enough time in the day, or money in your pocket. Do you have a practiced self-assurance that no matter which lane of the freeway you enter, it will always be the slowest one? Whatever we practice, we also creatively empower, whether it be a positive or a negative. After all, we are creating our lives. Exactly how do we do that? One moment at a time; one practice at a time.

It is essential that we practice right relationship with what we are creating. If you want to create a new response to something in your life, if you want to create enlightenment from ignorance, then you have to give that your attention, imagine it, and then practice it. Developing an enlivened alignment with strong, vibrant creativity will ensure that you will have that skill when you need it. And let's face it. As long as you find yourself in a body, on the Earth, you are going to find that on more than one occasion, a creative response comes in real handy. The bottom line is that you cannot expect to have or to enjoy the benefit of anything you never practice. This means you have to practice being creative, simply for the sake of being creative . . . to have creativity on tap.

So the next time you grab your surfboard and head for the ocean, or take out a musical instrument that has been collecting dust in the closet, or put on your gardening clothes and hat, please remember you are practicing keeping creativity alive and well in your life. That way, the next time life throws a curve ball your way, and it will, you will have the well-practiced and savvy ability to see yourself knocking that ball right out of the park.

You are the treasure you seek!

A Wilde Perspective on $pirituality and Money

*W*ell over one hundred years ago, the great Spiritual teacher and literary genius, Oscar Wilde, after visiting America, wrote, "Americans know the price of everything and the value of nothing." Oscar Wilde's wisdom, insight and penchant for truth are as accurate and sobering now as they were over ten decades ago. Okay, so maybe nowadays even the idea that we recognize the "price of everything" seems to be legitimately in question. But the "value" side seems to have deteriorated even more! Do we recognize the value of spending more time with our children or loved ones, or reading a book? We may see the value in personal accomplishments or being productive and "getting things done", but then again, we're talking about ego-based value . . . not exactly the "value" Oscar had in mind. I suspect that if he were here to visit us now, he would find these same words damning us with faint praise.

So, where and how did our value sensibilities get so polluted, diluted and distorted? Could it be that there is a connection between understanding our own Spiritual worth and power, and how we perceive the value and power of money? Another Wilde quote that takes us closer to this idea is, "Ordinary riches can be stolen; real riches cannot. In your soul are infinitely precious things that cannot be taken from you." How many of us relate to ourselves, and value ourselves as infinitely precious? How many of us correlate our power with our Spiritual identity, of being pure Love and nothing else? I suspect that most of us relate to ourselves in the same way that we would a commodity: that any value, power and worth we claim is the sum total of our materiali$tic po$$e$$ions and our earning potential. From our perspective, if it wasn't earned, deserved and bestowed upon us, it has no value. When the truth of the matter is, that as Divine Love, we do not have value, power and worth, we *are* value power and worth. And no one and no thing on the planet, has the power to change that. Deserving and worthy is not even an issue. It never has been, and never really will be, because we do not have it, we *are* it.

If we have not realized our own true authentic oneness with value, power and worth, is it any real surprise that relationships outside ourselves, being less intimate then the one we have with ourselves, lack clarity and explicitness? If we do not recognize our own value, power and worth, will we not simply project that ignorance out on to everything else in our lives? Then, whatever manifests outside of us, especially that which represents value, power and worth, takes the brunt of that perspective perversion: I barely make enough money to pay my bills . . . I have no value; I lost my job . . . I have no power; I didn't get the promotion . . . I have no worth. Or conversely, I made partner at the firm . . . I have value; I just bought a new BMW . . . I have power; I won the lottery . . . I have worth. What messages are we sending to ourselves about what is infinitely precious, and how does that affect our connection to the other aspects of our lives?

Oscar Wilde also said, "Life is too important to be taken seriously." Could it be that he is right? Could it be that we take life far too seriously, and that we are far too flippant and superficial in our consideration of our Divinity? How might our relationship to money and ourselves change if we valued the evolution of our Soul with the same diligence and commitment that we managed our $tock portfolio? Oscar Wilde was so wise about the human condition, he used to say, "Moderation is a fatal thing. Nothing succeeds like excess." And that certainly sums up our relationship with money, even if your name isn't Bill Gates. Enough never seems to be enough. So much of our daily focus of attention is wrapped up and intertwined with our relationship to money. If we were enough within ourselves, would that point of reference change how we feel about money? Would that make a radical difference in our ability to manifest it, hold on to it and to use it wisely? Is the solution to our money issues going to be found within us, or outside of us? I'm sure most of you are thinking, "Gee Vaishāli, I'm not sure either. Give me a couple of million dollars, time to enjoy it, and I'll get back to you."

Although Oscar had a privileged upbringing, he lived through stresses most of us would find unbearable. One of the many brilliant things about Oscar Wilde's life was his talent to maintain a pristine sense of humor no matter what life threw at him. He was unconditionally wise. He had many financial roller-coaster rides in his lifetime, and what he learned from that was, "Anyone who lives within their means suffers from a lack of imagination." The English government confiscated all of his assets and personal property and threw him in jail. After being released from prison, he died in poverty. However, Oscar never lost sight of his Divinity or his ability to take life lightly. He was very ill before he died and suffered great physical pain. He used to say, "I am so poor, I cannot even afford to die. Alas, I am dying beyond my means."

I know I have raised more questions than answers in this examination of money and Spirituality, so in closing let me leave you with one more final Oscar Wilde jewel of wisdom: "When I was young I thought that money was the most important thing in life; now that I am old I know that it is". He was the master of insight, and the master of the facetious. I think that says it all.

Rebel With or Without a Cause

Can you give us a little background information about yourself?

*I*n this life, I apparently signed up to be a teacher of unconditional love. The unconditional love instructor curriculum turned out to be a real bitch. You would not believe the final exam. And the graduate course work, for me, involved a plethora of exceptional challenges to work through. I passed, and hopefully the continuing education courses will be easier.

It all started at birth, as most beginnings do. I was born with several birth defects in the left eye. The eye had a cataract the size of a small planet - too large to be removed. As a matter of fact, I am still packing that baby around with me to this day. That eye also had a condition that caused it to turn extremely inward to the right. It would turn so severely inward that you could not see the iris or pupil at all. I appeared to have one very bright blue eye and one totally white eye. Needless to say the Cyclops look has never been very popular for winning friends or beauty contests. Many days, as a child, I remember being assaulted with rocks by my classmates. I became alienated due to unfashionable physical packaging.

My parents divorced when I was a small child. My mother remarried a man who shared the same commitment to alcohol consumption my mother enjoyed. When one parent drinks, life is rough. When both parents drink, there is no safe place. I remember getting out of bed and hiding when I heard them return home from an evening out. If they can't find you, they can't hit you. It is nice to know that even at the age of five, I could outsmart them.

By the time I was eight, due to lack of parental supervision, I was a total failure in school. One of my teachers took me aside and taught me how to read, write and speak properly. I made her my mother figure. Two years later she was brutally murdered by someone who wanted to make it look like a satanic, ritualistic homicide. I was so traumatized by the event that I suppressed the memory of ever knowing her. A few years later the police caught the alleged murderer. It was only then that I realized I had blotted out her memory in order to deal with the stress.

I have been lied to and cheated on by almost every intimate partner. One even threatened to kill me. He accused me of being a witch who had put a curse on him, because somehow I made it harder for him to cheat on me. He wanted me to suffer deeply for that. Talk about whack jobs!

I have been diagnosed terminal twice - once from an illness and once from injuries from a car accident. That's what I call "overkill". These events came with years of pain that make you want to end it all. The car accident injuries were disputed, and, of course, I lost the legal trial. I became the proud owner of over thirty thousand dollars in medical bills plus all the legal fees. After four years of not being able to work, I went through all my life savings. I still required medical treatment, and my physical condition made me unemployable. I suffered from constant nausea as a result of the injuries. For the first four years after the accident, it was difficult to sleep more than three hours a night. The migraine headaches were the worst of the tortures, sometimes lasting more than twenty straight hours. The headaches made the nausea intensify, and at 5' 6" I got down to ninety-four pounds. Trust me, it was not a fashionable ninety-four pounds. While this was in progress, I went through a nasty, two year, drawn out divorce. This was one learning curve I hope never to repeat.

You come across as so positive and playful. Are most people surprised to find that your life has been so difficult?
Oh, yeah. I recall a recent radio interview about my life. We had barely covered the childhood stress, violence and first terminal diagnosis when the interviewer said, "Well it is incredible you are still alive!" My response was. . . . "Well there is more, we've actually just started." I usually do not go into much detail about my life, because, well quite frankly, there is usually not enough time in any program to fit in even the highlights . . . or the low lights as the case may be. Besides, I feel that what I have learned from my life is much more important to share than how I came about learning it.

What triggered the tempering amidst all these challenges?
The big turning point came when I learned of the 18th century Swedish scientist/mystic Emanuel Swedenborg. At the time, I was in my mid-twenties and was diagnosed terminal from an illness.

Swedenborg first originated the phrase, "You are what you love, and you love whatever you give your attention to." In other words, your awareness is love, and whatever you are giving your attention to, is also what you love. Since love is the most powerful force in the universe, when you give something your attention, you are imbuing it with love. Love is wholeness making. Whatever you give your love to, you will bring more of it into the whole of your life. This means if you love something limited, you will bring more limitation into the whole of your life. If you love what is unlimited, you will experience more unlimiting things.

Because of the difficulties life delivered early on to my doorstep, I gave worry the bulk of my attention. Worry was my drug of choice. It was the first thing I would focus on when I got up in the morning; it was the last thing I thought about before going to sleep at night. I mainlined worry. I was constantly asking, "What else can go wrong?" instead of, "what else can go right?" My love of worry brought more to worry about into the whole of my life.

Swedenborg taught me that what we give out attention to in the physical world affects where we live Spiritually. If I did not want to live in a Spiritually hellishly limiting place, then I needed to realize there was nothing in it for me to give my attention to anything limited.

Once I understood the cause and effect around worry — the more I worried, the more I would manifest something to worry about — I was then able to stop the snowball from turning into an avalanche and give my attention to more empowering things. Before Swedenborg, I felt justified in my hyper-attention to worry. After Swedenborg, I realized there was no justification for giving one's attention to anything limited . . . unless you want to learn more about limitation, by bringing more of it into your life.

Breaking the worry addiction was a major turning point in my life. Without Swedenborg's wisdom, I do not know how I would have seen that. When you are buried alive by life's lessons, that is actually when you can *least* afford to entertain anything limiting with your attention. It is not the time to be empowering the stress with the momentum of your attention, your love for it.

What else did you learn that changed your health status, as you clearly did not die, did you?
No, not that time. I am saving that for a later occasion. But there were plenty of days I felt like I was sitting in God's waiting room. It was also at that time that I started studying Indian Ayurveda, Tibetan Ayurveda and Chinese Medicine. I felt my culture was not offering me what I needed to deal holistically with the health issues I was facing. What I learned from those ancient healing sciences is that our thoughts, emotions, experiences and perceptions travel through our digestive tract in the exact same fashion that our food does, because these intangibles *are* a form of food. The same processes that happen in the digestion of physical food happen in the digestion of "human experience" food. That means that the first thing one has to do with their thoughts, emotions, perceptions and experiences is to be able to swallow them. Then one has to be able to stomach them, and pull from them what one needs to become a stronger, more compassionate, awakened person. The final step is to let the rest go for the waste in our lives that it is.

I realized that as a result of the accumulation of the earlier stresses in my life, and my habit of obsessively worrying about what was going to happen next as a response to that stress, I was feeding my body a steady diet of stagnant, life-depleting energy - food it could not digest or eliminate properly.

Swedenborg created an inner revolution in my life. Because of the Spiritual Law, "You are what you love, and you love whatever you give your attention to," I was able to understand the cause and effect between what I was giving my attention to, and therefore my love to, and the degenerative illness the body was suffering from. No wonder my body was withering away, and I did not have a life worth living. What I was habituated to giving my attention to was sucking the life right out me, literally!

I also learned a rare form of self-administered Chinese internal organ massage. Energetically, it is like performing an emotional exorcism. After years of cleaning up my thoughts, refining my diet and pulling out the stagnant emotional energy from my body, I made a full recovery. It took years of consistent, steady, dedicated practice. I did not get in that condition overnight, and it could not be resolved overnight. Pain, however, is a great source of inspiration. And apparently I was a slow learner.

You write a great deal in your book about the power of what you practice. Did you learn that from the recovery process?
Absolutely! I learned that what we know intellectually can be deceiving. Just because we think something, we are then under the impression we know it. I have found that not to be true. What you *live*, is what you really know, and you are living whatever you have practiced. I often watch *The Dr. Phil Show*. When he has a guest on that is suffering as a result of some practiced behavior/perception in his life, Dr. Phil frequently asks his guest, "You know what you are doing is harmful or self destructive?" The guest always acknowledges that they are fully aware that what they are doing is not healthy. They understand in their heads that what they are doing is not helping them. But that changes nothing, because what they really *know* is what they live. And what they live is what they have practiced. Knowing something does not mean we make better choices or live a better life. Changing what you live, what you practice, however, changes everything.

I have found the power of practice is more influential than any drug. The force of habit has a momentum all its own, regardless of whether or not it is useful and serving. The more I practice watching what I love with my awareness, the easier it becomes, and the better I get at recognizing and releasing limited thoughts and perceptions. Simply starting and establishing this practice is the most profound part of liberating your mind and life through the Spiritual Law "You are what you love and you love whatever you give your attention to."

Do you have any specific advice for other women who share a similar background and challenges as you?
The first thing I want to say is that being cheated on and struggling with feelings of worthlessness and powerlessness is not just a female issue, it is a human experience issue that recognizes no gender boundary. With that said, I understand the female experience and the subtle and insidious ways women have a habit of tying their value, power and worth to their looks, relationships and their ability to please others. That's what I call "the good girl" complex.

Having been born with a physical birth defect that left me feeling damaged and defective for the first 20 plus years of my life, I really get this one. What I have learned from that experience, as well as the illness and injury I struggled to recover from, is that we human beings are *NOT* our bodies. Our awareness has an intimate relationship with our bodies, so we are intimately aware of what our bodies are going through. But we are not our packaging; we are our Spiritual Identity.

It is very helpful to talk positively and lovingly to the body. Tell the body you love it, you honor it, and that you trust it has the wisdom and power to heal what is needed. Getting angry with the body and telling it that it is too fat or unacceptable only confuses the body. If you tell the body, "I have a big butt" the body will think that is what you want, and it will go out of its way to give you that result, because you have identified it as "self."

As Spiritual Beings having a human experience, we do not have value, power and worth . . . we *are* value, power and worth. And no one and no thing on this planet has the power to change that. Oftentimes we disenfranchise ourselves from connecting to that reality via what we give our attention to. We have free will. We decide if we want to love aligning with our true nature by exclusively giving that story our attention. Or we can use our free will to take us down a road that tells us the outer world has the prerogative to determine our value, power and worth – not a pretty picture.

It is common knowledge that establishing and cultivating relationships is how women are hardwired. Women, like men, want to be loved and respected. How women go about that, however, can be very different from men. My experience shows that a high percentage of women develop an inner "good girl." The inner "good girl" wants to make others happy, wants to establish value, power and worth by being the people pleaser. Many women overextend themselves, because they cannot say, "No." The inner "good girl" prohibits that. Many mothers have no sense of balance in their lives; they meet everyone else's needs and put their own needs so far down the list, they never, or rarely get acknowledged. This is my suggestion on how to handle the inner "good girl." The next time she rears her "I'm not important; I have to make others happy; what will others think of me if I do not perform what they want from me," take her out to the backyard and simply shoot her in the head and be done with her. If you don't have a backyard, throw her off the balcony.

The "good girl" has more lives than Bill Murray in Groundhog Day. She has a nasty habit of resurrecting immediately, because most women are highly invested and very well practiced at giving her life. But she *can* eventually be put to rest. We practiced giving her a voice, and we can practice taking that voice away. What is imperative is that we realize *when* we are giving away our power through the "good girl", in exchange for love and acceptance. Remember, we do not have love; we *are* love. Love is not a commodity to be bargained or leveraged. When women claim their power as the force of Divine Love they are, the need to sublimate their true and authentic needs and feelings for the "good girl" agenda resolves itself.

That is the beauty of aligning one's attention with the truth — it sets us free. This is, in fact, how we get honest and real about what we are giving our attention to: if it is not setting us free, we have not yet seen the truth. And when we do give our attention to the truth about our value, power, worth and inseparable oneness with Divine Love, we *know* it, because it sets us free. Free, free, Lord Almighty, free at last!

Peace of Cake

*T*here is a Spiritual Law that is expressed as follows: "As it is above, so it is below; as it is within, so it is without." The best way to understand this Law is to imagine that the Spiritual world is organized by what its inhabitants love... by their affections. Higher realms love Divine Love and Wisdom, sharing, seeing everyone equally as God, and being of service. Lower realms love lying, cheating, stealing, superior/inferior, manipulation, greed, cruelty. Each is organized according to what it loves. As it is above, so it is below. Now imagine that our inner perspectives, values and affinities get projected out from the hidden invisible interior, onto the visible, physically tangible exterior world. As it is within, so it is without.

This Spiritual Law makes realizing and living Spiritual qualities very interesting. One such Spiritual quality is peace. Peace could be on the endangered species list, considering how rare the appearance of a living peace seems to be on this planet. It is, therefore, no wonder that the commonly held notions about it are extremely pedestrian and stay completely sequestered from our Spiritual Law. So how do we go about catching a glimpse of it within and without? The mirror or reflective intelligence we are searching for in this examination is acceptance.

Without an inner action and valuing of acceptance, exterior peace in the world at large has no environment in which to exist.

It would be like trying to support human life in the vacuum of space. It simply isn't going to happen; it violates all the laws of Nature. The conundrum is that internalized acceptance is just as rare as Earthly manifested peace.

So what is authentic acceptance and why is it that peace cannot manifest without it? Acceptance is the foundation of all tolerance and compassion. It is the intelligence that allows tolerance and compassion to take root in our hearts and minds. Acceptance is inclusion of others. Acceptance values others' right to exist and to express themselves. Without accepting that your neighbor is equally God and sacred, peace hasn't a prayer, literally, figuratively, or metaphorically.

Albert Einstein said it best, "We cannot simultaneously prepare for war and peace." War is divisive. It separates us from one another. It is an extreme action driven by an attitude of non-acceptance. Peace, on the other hand, is inclusive. It is embracing. It is an acknowledgment of mutually agreed upon acceptance. War and peace cannot co-exist, as one would simply cancel out the other. No one can be accepting and tolerant of the other guy and be declaring war on him at the same time.

As for our "as it is within, so it is without" Law, this would mean that in order for us as a people, a nation, a planet, to actualize peace as a reality, that action must first begin within each of us individually. It must have an interior basis and origin before it can show up as an outer expression. Peace is not going to happen as a result of some perfectly executed foreign policy. Peace on Earth is not the result of taking an exterior hand and re-arranging exterior geographical furniture. Peace on Earth is the reflection of an inner attitude that is aligned with acceptance.

Peace is inseparable from the "as it is within, so it is without" Law of cause and effect.

No government can legislate acceptance. It is an inner regulation, not an outer enforceable law. If we are not seeing peace rearing its Heavenly head in the world around us, then it must certainly be equally as absent from our inner lives as well.

If we were accepting first of ourselves, of the life lessons that find us and of our reactions to them, then we would certainly be experiencing a more peaceful reality. Now here comes the tricky part: to catch ourselves when we are not inclusive of the whole of our lives. Empowering inner self-acceptance arrests our tyrannizing habit to criticize. When we are self-accepting we are not violently self-critical. As it is above with war and peace, so it is here below with accepting and critical. One is exchanged for the other.

Peace must begin inside each of us. We cannot live or extend anything to another human being that we lack direct knowledge of ourselves. Once an attitude of acceptance for "what is" has the opportunity to be cultivated and nurtured within us, it can then begin to circulate into our relationships with others and finally to the world at large. With every self-acceptance victory we claim, we strengthen our ability to extend that same acceptance to others and the life lessons they find themselves embroiled in. Eventually the practice of acceptance would possess the communities, countries, and global networks we all share. We would all become infected with peace, embodying that peace within and without.

If every time we became aware of our own lack of acceptance, we could then correlate that personal sabotaging with the erosion of peace in the world around us, we could turn the global tide. World peace gets another advocate every time we stop in the midst of our own critical diatribe and ask ourselves, "Is this war on peace really what I want to do with my attention and energy?" We must value waking up from where we run on autopilot, defaulting to harsh judgments against ourselves and others. The good news is that we do not have to wait for anyone else to implement peace on Earth. It is not up to the major corporations, elected officials, or religious leaders to give peace a chance. It is up to each of us, in every present moment, to remember, "as it is within, so it is without."

Whether or not you agree with these suggested inner evolutionary practices, please consider that all I am saying is give acceptance a chance. Who knows. The mind you make peace with may be your own. Oh, and one last point. This Spiritual Law does not apply if you live in Las Vegas. What happens in Las Vegas stays in Las Vegas, or as it is within, so it is . . . within? But then that's a whole other story altogether.

Section 2 ~
Personal Transformation

Don't Take It Personally

*I*n Taiwan there is a device known as a Taiwanese monkey trap. It is a simple box made of open wooden slats. A banana is placed inside the box, and it is clearly visible through the open slats. There is a hole in the box just large enough for a monkey's open hand to reach through. Once the monkey has a grip on the banana, the trap is sprung. The monkey now finds the hole is too small for a closed fist clutching a banana to pass back out again. There is actually nothing holding the monkey in the trap - except for its attachment to the banana. The monkey will stand there, one arm in the box firmly clutching the banana, for hours, even days. The monkey will remain there until the trappers return to bag the poor distressed creature easily, for the monkey will not relinquish its grip on the banana.

Before you laugh too hard at the monkey's behavior, consider that all human beings have much in common with both the monkey, as well as the trap. How could we, the vastly superior beings, possibly be emulating this ludicrous creature, you ask? Well, once we get our perceptual grip on something, we oftentimes will not let go of it to save our lives. For us 'more advanced' monkeys, the wooden, open-slat box corresponds to a life of suffering, and taking things personally is the banana. As long as we have a death grip on taking everything in life personally, we're caught in a life of suffering and limitation. Basically, we are trapped by our mind - our thoughts and beliefs. If we would only open up our perception, we could then release what is holding us hostage, to our detriment and discomfort.

According to Vedic psychology, what most of us are experiencing as personal events are not even personal. They are universal, but once again our perception gets in the way. It may not be personal, but we "take it personally," as *my* banana. For example, air, fire and water are all universal elements. We all universally experience them. So, when was the last time you saw someone running around, holding their breath in a constant inhale, informing all around them, "This is my air! My air! You just wouldn't understand it, because it is my air!" Most likely never. We would immediately recognize such behavior as misplaced identification, and move as rapidly as possible away from the deluded offensive party.

So it is with taking life personally; it is misplaced identification. Vedic psychology says you do not have to take their word for it, you can prove it to yourself. Just ask yourself, "Like air, fire and water, were emotions around before you showed up on the planet?" Were human experiences happening before your charming butt arrived to grace the third rock from the sun? Did you invent thought, or was that bouncing around long before you were born? If it was on the planet before you showed up, then it is a universal event, and there is nothing personal about it.

Emanuel Swedenborg says the same about the human experience. He says that as a spiritual creature we take a physical form and come to the universal schoolhouse called the planet Earth. Swedenborg says we do this because this universal classroom is the fastest, most efficient way for us to educate ourselves about our Divinity. Swedenborg goes on to say that if there were a faster more effective way to realize our mind than the universal Earth classroom, then we would be there, experiencing that something else. Therefore the opportunity to free the mind is offered universally, to everyone, at all times throughout the whole of history. And the educational process that this entails is also offered universally, to all peoples, at all times. Whatever this reality is on earth, it is not personal. What it is, is universally lived, shared and Divinely designed as a collective phenomenon.

The real insidious side effect of distilling universal life into the personal is that it destroys all perceptual balance. Responding to the whole of life with an equal and even mindset is how the Eastern philosophies define balanced perception. Taking the movement of life personally skews that balance, by either elevating the scales high into self-aggrandizing and egoistic self indulgence, or by unbalancing the scale in the complete opposite direction by plummeting perception into victimhood - helpless and hopeless self pity. Who has not cast the first 'taking it personally' stone, or grabbed their own 'taking it personally' banana, with a story like, "I knew it; as soon as I get in this line, it slows down." Or, "why does the stock market wait until I make an investment before going into a free fall?" All of us, every single last one of us has to find a way to free ourselves from the burden our personal perceptions have created. The 'taking it personally' stories we create with our perceptions, keep us trapped in our self-inflicted Taiwanese monkey trap. Honestly, unless we are completely enlightened and fully liberated, we are all held hostage, imprisoned by the invisible bars of our own perceptual construction, with our paw firmly around that elusive banana.

We have to learn a new habit: open the personal perceptual fist that has become so tightly closed around that 'taking it personally' banana, and to move freely into the universal world, which simultaneously lives and thrives all around us. Only our relentless attachment to perceiving things as a personal event holds us in this limited place of suffering, while a greater choice is always available to us, inviting us to let go of the personal one, and move freely forward, empowered as a universal one – the all-powerful, perpetual plantain.

How do we keep from projecting our own personal story out onto everything that shows up in our lives? How do we refrain from internalizing the insensitive "others" in our lives that feel the need to spoon-feed us harsh judgments and criticisms as if it were mother's milk? How do we keep from repeating over and over in our heads the mean-spirited relationships and hurtful events that we feel are the cause and source of our suffering? How do we take the "personal" out of our personal experience of life? To quote Hamlet, "That is the rub!"

Taking things personally damages our universal vision. It contracts our perception of self into a very small and narrow point in time. It limits and restricts our sight; it misguides our higher inclusive wisdom. When reliving the injuries incurred along the path of life, we forget that this is but one small segment of an infinitely larger journey. We become amnesic to the reality that these events are the tempering forces that break our hearts open and offer us the gift of loving larger. These personal affronts are how we evolve into one who chooses to love like they have never been hurt before. These "plantain" perpetrators of pain in our lives have come to offer us the opportunity to grow beyond the limits of our stories, of our ego likes and dislikes, of the fragility of the temporal world. *Life is a gift, learning is the challenge, evolving is the purpose.*

We have all been brainwashed to think and believe we are our experiences, our thoughts, our bodies. The Eastern-based spiritual traditions, such as Buddhism, would like to remind us differently. We, as spiritual beings, are eternal, permanent and unchanging. Anything that is impertinently impermanent and subject to change, such as fashion, bodies, weather, teen idols, favorite television programs, the Dow Jones Industrial Average, menstrual cycles, political structures, boxers versus briefs, thoughts and emotions, cannot by virtue of their variable nature, be true self. We are beyond anything that we have been labeling and investing in as personal. We are awareness itself. That is our spiritual identity. The temporal world comes and goes; it gyrates and fluctuates. We, as the observer of these movements, are the eternal, invariable portion of the equation. Awareness is our universal, true self; it is what we bring with us to the human experience, and what we take with us when we leave. The human experience is the vehicle, the classroom through which we, as Divine consciousness, get to experience ourselves as awareness, as the force of eternal love we authentically are, to the exclusion of everything else.

If there is validity to the hundredth monkey theory, * then it is indeed time we all taught ourselves to let go of the banana and simply walk away from the misguided "personal" into the expansive universal. For that is our birthright; that is what we are divinely designed for, and that is where the truth that sets us free will at last be found.

Oh, and now that my hand is out of the trap, I'll have the banana split . . . to go.

* The hundredth monkey theory: When enough individuals in a population adopt a new idea or behavior, there occurs an ideo-

logical breakthrough that allows the new awareness to be communicated directly from mind to mind without connection of external experience and then *all* individuals in the population spontaneously adopt it. This may be one of the many ways we create reality with our perception on a collective level. It may be that when enough of us hold something to be true, it becomes true for everyone.

Good and Evil: It Is a Matter of Perspective

When approaching the concepts of good and evil, I define good as unlimited and freeing, and evil as limited and confining. But just how limiting or how extensive? As with most mental concepts, your mileage may vary. The truth is that good and evil are just different points on the same line of consciousness. So what separates these points on the line? Perspective. And what determines perspective? Free will. So it is impossible to tackle the idea of good and evil without acknowledging the power of perspective and the issue of free will.

Emanuel Swedenborg defined a Spiritual Law by the phrase, "You are what you love, and you love whatever you are giving your attention to." What do you love giving your attention to? Do you love giving your attention to only what is unlimited and expansive? Or do you still entertain the notion that there is some payoff in your justification to empower what is limiting with your focus? When giving your attention to something like, "I do not have enough time," or "I do not have enough money," that may not seem "evil" in the traditional way we label something as evil. But just ask yourself if those statements *feel* limiting when you give them your attention. Do they produce a limited response in your life and nervous system? Does your world feel constricting?

We have a tendency of relating to evil as something way less pervasive in our lives than what we give our attention to. We like to see it as a description we are most comfortable attaching to serial killers, the IRS, Fox News Network, and Austin Powers' nemesis, Dr. Evil. But what exactly is evil, when we separate it from an action? It is a limiting, fear-based thought that someone, through their own free will, is giving their attention to.

All Spiritual Traditions speak of the power of free will. Free will reigns on this planet. The Divine has seen fit to Bless everyone with the free will to decide for themselves what they will do with their attention. There are no programmed human robots on this planet. We are free to give our attention to the love side of the equation, which we have defined as unlimited in nature. But that action only has value if we are also free *not* to give our attention to love. That other choice would be fear, which we have equally defined as evil and limiting in action and consequences.

Swedenborg has a great definition of Heaven and hell. He describes Heaven as a place or state of being that is unlimited, and hell as a place or state of being that is limited. That is why when we worry or devote our attention to other equally limiting thoughts, our life can feel so hellish. There is a pattern that clearly begins to emerge here: the relationship between good and evil, love and fear, and Heaven and hell, Austin Powers and Dr. Evil.

When we freely choose a love-based thought that feels good, right and liberating, our life takes on an unlimited Heavenly quality. When we freely surrender our attention to fear-based thoughts that constrict and contract our existence, our experience of life becomes hellishly limited and unhappy.

The real question here is where will you choose to live on this good/evil continuum, this realm of freely cultivated perspective? Do you understand that when you give your attention to fear-based thoughts, you are edging your way across the invisible line of consciousness to the side that evil occupies? Conversely, do you enjoy the personal empowerment that is derived from committing your attention to only what is unlimiting and freeing in nature, co-creating the manifestation of Heaven on Earth, thus keeping you solidly on the love-based side of our ethereal line of consciousness?

The truth of the matter is that we go back and forth as our focus changes moment to moment. But we learn from each side. We do appear to be rather slow learners here in the planet Earth schoolroom, as we seem to freely allow a backsliding from the love side to the fear side with Olympic quality agility. We migrate unceasingly between Heaven and hell. On a daily basis we suffer horribly from evil thoughts turned into action, but we also heal and liberate our minds and lives with good and useful thoughts. Hopefully, when we keep the imaginary continuum in mind, it will help our consciousness learning curve.

Time has been defined as nothing more than a change of perspective. So something can be both good and evil, depending on *when* we give it our attention, and whether we are coming from our hearts, that expansive place of love, or the ego, that limited place of fear. Remember that "good" little band of outlaws called The Taliban? We financed and armed them to fight the "evil" empire of the Soviet Union when they invaded Afghanistan. Then the cold war ended; Russia was no longer our enemy. Oops! Didn't we also arm Iraq, the 'good" guys, to fight the "evil" religious fanatics in Iran? Hey, weren't those our weapons that Iraq used against us in the Gulf war, after they invaded Kuwait? How are we supposed to know when the U.S government moves from good to evil; from love to fear; from their hearts to their heads; from Heaven to hell? Is there a government agency that keeps track of all this? If, so let's pray it is run by our good pal, Austin Powers, and not Dr. Evil or mini me.

There's more than one way to slay a dragon.

Laughing Matters

*E*ver look up humor in the dictionary? Don't. The punch line is forgettable, and the set-up is predictable. But what is this mystery we call humor? What is it about humor that makes the unbearable, well . . . bearable? As the brilliant Oscar Wilde said about death, at the end of his life when he was homeless and penniless, "I am dying beyond my means." "I did not know it was such a pain to die; I thought that life had taken all the agonies to itself." And about the rundown hotel he was dying in at the time, "My wall paper and I are fighting a duel to the death. Either the wallpaper goes or I do!" So what is it about humor that makes Oscar's unspeakable pain . . . well, hilarious?

"Dying is easy, comedy is hard." Sir Donald Wolfit, British actor and director.

Whatever humor is, I never want to live in a world without it. In his biography, Mark Twain said, "Humor is mankind's greatest blessing." Not being one to argue with Mark Twain, I would have to agree for a number of reasons. The first would be actor Alan Alda's observation about humor:

"When people are laughing, they're generally not killing one another." Already a winning position for humor, above and beyond politics. The second would be that without humor, we would have no defense against suffering, the anal retentive, or the morbidly serious.

Perhaps I know why it is man alone who laughs: He alone suffers so deeply that he had to invent laughter. - Friedrich Nietzsche

In a scene from *Annie Hall*, Woody Allen's mother takes him to a psychiatrist, because he has stopped doing his homework. When the doctor asks the younger version of Allen why he has stopped engaging in life, the response Allen provides is that he has read that the Universe is continually expanding and will one day rip apart. So what is the point? "Tell him the Universe is none of his business!" Allen's well-intentioned Mother implores the doctor to inform her over intellectualizing offspring. Why is this so funny? Maybe the question would be better asked, "Why not?" Or as Woody Allen, perhaps in anticipation of this very question said, "Eternal nothingness is fine if you happen to be dressed for it."

Four out of three people are bad at fractions. – Milton Einstein, (a distance cousin of Albert's)

I suspect it is author James Thurber who best answers this question, "The wit makes fun of other persons; the satirist makes fun of the world; the humorist makes fun of himself. But in doing so, he identifies himself with people – that is, people everywhere, not for the purpose of taking them apart, but simply revealing their true nature." Humor has a way of equalizing life's playing field, while simultaneously exposing our naked truths for all the world to see. As Victor Borge phrased it, "Laughter is the shortest distance between two people." Humor opens the mind and the heart. It allows for profound truths to find a way to seep into the more remote recesses of our lives, bypassing our need to defend and justify shallower points of view.

Oh, you hate your job? Why didn't you say so? There is a support group for that. It's called EVERYBODY, and they meet at the bar.
-Drew Carey

As a wise Spiritual Teacher once said, "We have a tendency to take God lightly and life seriously, when we should be taking our Divinity seriously and life lightly." Or as William Zinser remarked, "I want to make people laugh - so they will begin to see things seriously." Ah yes, humor, the inventor of the power of a paradox, or as I like to say it, "The ability to achieve total heavyosity with complete lightness; the flexibility to perceive one's own suffering as a source of never ending amusement." I remember asking a friend of mine who lost both legs in a freak accident if he always had his penetrating sense of humor, or if it was aroused as a survival technique after the accident. His response surprised me. He said, "Well, life really isn't worth living is it . . . if you can't laugh at it at the end of the day." Most people would have been pre-occupied with the reality that they would never walk again. However, my friend's sense of humor was still completely intact, and he was not going to compromise the power of laughter moving him forward.

If I had no sense of humor, I would long ago have committed suicide.
- Gandhi

Will Rogers once said, "An onion can make people cry, but there has never been a vegetable invented to make them laugh." I suspect that is why life's challenges were created: to keep us all knee deep and rich in comic material. As Max Beerbohm pointed out, "Nobody ever died of laughter." Which leads me to suspect it is the best antidote for limitation and suffering we have. I know laughter has been my insulation against the firestorm of life. While still in high school, I remember another young woman caught me playing puppets with my pencil and eraser, making them dance and sing across my desktop. "You know what I most admire about you?" She said with a totally straight face, "your ability to unconditionally entertain yourself." I have never forgotten that moment of self-realization, and I shall be eternally grateful for her observation.

The only rules comedy can tolerate are those of taste, and the only limitations those of libel. - James Thurber

And for those who have read this article and already incorporated it in their everyday lives . . . I leave you with this:

Students achieving Oneness will move on to Twoness. - Woody Allen

R-E-S-P-E-C-T
Find Out What It Means to Me

*T*oday we have to pay attention to a wide spectrum of politically correct agendas - our PC-sensitive etiquette realities. Do you still say "handicapped" as the parking placards state, or do you say "physically challenged"? God forbid you refer to an airline employee as a "stewardess". The last stewardess retired over 20 years ago. The airlines now only employ "flight attendants." As if the PC jargon were not restricting enough, the new improved PC behavior boundaries need to be observed as well. The biggest behavioral boundary that has reared its cosmetically challenged (i.e. ugly) head is: what is Spiritually mature behavior and what is not? When do you draw a line in the sand, and when do you turn the other cheek?

Recently I was talking with a businessman who was dealing with members of the "Spiritual Community". He was greatly shocked by their materialistic, egocentric behavior. "These people are supposed to be better than this!" he complained, with a quality of bitterness that comes with disappointment in what he had clearly anticipated would be a better world. "Quite, frankly, I'm shocked that you're shocked!" I told him. After all people are people, no matter what community they profess membership to. We need to look no further than Sister Geneva's Psychic Hotline service (or any televangelist) to find gleaming examples of blinding human frailty.

Just because your livelihood advertises a higher, loftier standard of human conduct does not mean, as a human being, you will suddenly shed all your imperfections and never again act like a self-absorbed child. Spiritual creatures come to the Earth to practice and explore growing beyond what is limiting, life-destructive and diminishing. The stuff (i.e. excrement) we are here to grow beyond needs a place in which to show up, so that we can practice putting it down and choosing something else. We are all excrementally challenged, or we wouldn't be here. My first suggestion is make your peace with the excrement (i.e. sh*t) hitting the fan; that is why the Earth was created. Here we have a place to work out our issues, without messing up the rest of the Universal "neighborhood". If you resist the purpose behind the creation of the entire physical realm, it will most likely screw up your afternoon, not to mention your life. So, get over it. There are no short cuts in the Tao. We all get the whole of life — the tolerable, as well as the intolerable.

Now that we have established the ground breaking reality that people are less than "ideally perfect" (i.e. have issues with just about everything), and always will be as long as they are coming here to learn and grow, what is the best way to respond to this ongoing annoying situation? Jesus tells us to "Love our enemies." (So does Hallmark. The card people say it keeps them confused.) That is great advice, and I do not have an issue with it . . . but that does not always mean I know how to be aligned with that wisdom. Does "Love you enemies" mean becoming a doormat and letting people walk all over you, wiping their feet on your dreams? This is where being a member of a "Spiritual Community" becomes very tricky. How does one establish fair and healthy boundaries yet still remain "Christ like" or true to their "Buddha Nature"? The answer is somewhere between grabbing your shotgun in hand with "Kill the wabbit!" in your heart like Elmer Fudd, and passively letting Lucy pull the football out from under you every year, like Charlie Brown.

Balance is what we are essentially after in our relationships and in our lives. But even with balance we cannot necessarily control our relationships with other people. All we really have is sovereignty in our own lives. We can strive to achieve that balance by asking what is fair for all beings involved. We need to respect the Divinity of others as well as our own. When we die and experience what Dannion Brinkley calls our 'panoramic life review', where we sit down with God, a large popcorn and junior mints, and see the home movie of our life, we are going to have to be accountable for not only why we trashed the God in others, but also why we allowed the Divine within us to be treated as inferior and irrelevant.

Saying to others who are deeply challenged in the arena of playing nicely with others (i.e. as*holes), that they do not have our permission to "dis" the Divine in us, and that they are most welcome to take their toys and play elsewhere, is a loving and Spiritually appropriate action. Granted it needs to be executed with respect for all parties involved, but choosing not to allow people in your life who are toxic and ruinous is how you respect your Spiritual identity and relationship with Prime Source. You are allowed to have a backbone and still be tolerant, compassionate and clear. When you come face to face with God, you can say, "I feel good about how I valued and respected my Divinity, and I extended that openly and fairly to all other God creatures everywhere." The meek will inherit the Earth, but the happy, well balanced people who value respecting fair and healthy boundaries will inherit a life worth living while on the Earth!

THE MECHANICS OF
CONDEMNATION

Hiding Out with
Tolerance and Compassion

*T*olerance and compassion, like love, are words that have gotten a lot of mileage lately. It is both Buddhist and PC (politically correct) to advocate for T & C. But what do we really know about the power behind these words? Tolerance and compassion are not merely intellectual states of mind. They are meant to be embodied, shared, dare I say it . . . LIVED! Tolerance and compassion are divine forms of intelligence that invite us to require more of ourselves. We live in a world where we are accustomed to assigning blame as an immediate response to any situation. We have to know who dropped the ball; who's at fault? The greatest social shame would be something unacceptable happening on *your* watch! We live in a world where "I am right, and that gives me might!" Whatever happened to agreeing to disagree? Aren't right and wrong subjective forms of wisdom — different degrees of the same thing? When I say that, I'm not talking about right and wrong in serial killing, wife beating or child molesting. I'm talking about right and wrong in how one subjectively experiences reality.

Not too long ago, Linda Ronstadt, playing to a Las Vegas audience, demonstrated this point perfectly. Linda felt compelled to share her political views, her likes and dislikes, among elected personalities. The crowd's response for sharing her unsolicited views was nothing short of a riot . . . and I do not mean a laugh riot. The singer was incensed that the general public did not share her reality, and the general public was outraged that she occupied their time with her political opinions. That wasn't what they came to hear. Why celebrities insist on treating the general public like idiots who are unable to form their own viewpoint without the benefit of a star's "celestial" guidance has always confused me. But I usually chalk it up to they're being well intentioned, and let it go. After all, I know my own mind. If they have a different point of view than mine, who cares! On my deathbed, what Barbra Streisand thinks about the political climate of the Middle East is the last thing that will be dominating my focus of attention.

It has become so commonplace to perceive others as wrong or bad, because they exercise their free will in a different direction. I remember seeing an interview between Barbara Walters and Madonna. The Diva was going on and on about how she did not want the members of her audience to dress like her; she wanted them to *think* like her. Hey Madonna, can you say fascism? Making others think the way one person wants, contrary to what is in **their** hearts, is not exactly socially elevating. Everybody has to find his or her own way home. Everyone has to be able to grow in the direction and speed that they need to, not as rigidly pre-determine by a few privileged, self-appointed, select know-it-alls.

Where is the tolerance for the other guy's opinion? Where is the compassion for the learning experience and ideas of others? Who cares if someone on the A-list agrees with anyone else on the planet. When Albert Einstein was alive, hardly anyone agreed with where he was going in his understanding of time, matter and energy. Imagine Einstein being stifled because Clara Bow or Errol Flynn did not endorse his view of reality! What happened to the celebration of diversity of thought and imagination? What happened to treating others as you would want to be treated? If someone attempted to invalidate Madonna's viewpoint, solely based on a lack of like-mindedness, you know the Earth would shift on its axis from the explosion of unjust and unfair accusations Madonna would hurl back. Yet Madonna, with a straight face, can tell Walters she wants everyone else on the planet to think the same way she does. Are we not listening to ourselves?

What a dull, boring and limited world it would be if everyone thought, felt and saw the same way. There would be no ingenuity, no paradigm break throughs, and no advancement for the human Soul. There would be no Gandhi, no Martin Luther King Jr., no Princess Diana. Ralph Waldo Emerson would never have written about "Self Reliance." Shakespeare would never have allowed Polonius to utter those immortal words, "To thine own self be true." Jesus would never have stood up against the religious leaders of his time. The only free thinkers would be Homer Simpson and the kids at South Park.

It's no wonder adolescence is so traumatizing. That is when one needs to be accepted, because not "fitting in" is so socially painful. That is the time most critical in our development, when nonconformity crushes our psyche and soul so mercilessly. That's why we make Olympian heroes out of characters like "Cool Hand Luke" and James Dean's "Rebel Without A Cause"; they moved *against* the current of conformity. (And just for the record, Madonna and Linda, these iconic characters didn't think like you either! Oh, well!) We live in a free country. There is no caveat that it has to be free to think only what Madonna, Linda Ronstadt, George Bush or Dick Cheney want you to think.

Free will is a great gift. Imagine a world where others respected and valued the exercise of free will. Consider a world where it is more important to actualize your own free will, than it is to conform to another's agenda, no matter how vogue they may be. There used to be a saying you rarely hear these days, "I may not agree with what you have to say, but I would defend your right to say it with my life." Wouldn't it be interesting if that idea were as popular as being politically correct.

Oscar   **Oscar Wilde**

The Importance of Being Spiritually Wilde

or I Have Only My Wilde Spiritual Genius To Declare! or I wish I had an Oscar Wilde Demeanor!

When most people hear the name Oscar Wilde they are reminded of his unparalleled literary brilliance. The novel *The Picture of Dorian Grey* may come to mind, or perhaps one of Wilde's timeless, classic plays such as *The Importance of Being Earnest, A Woman of No Importance, Lady Windermere's Fan,* or *An Ideal Husband.* Maybe you are a fan of poetry, and you best remember Wilde for his dazzling artistic poems. Or you may know him from his wit, which is still frequently quoted today. It is easy to see why Oscar Wilde holds such an exalted place in 21st century literature. What most people do not know is that Oscar Wilde was as ahead of his time Spiritually, as he was intellectually. Oscar was, and still remains, the definition of what it means to be Spiritually Wilde!

> *"I have the simplest of tastes, I am always satisfied with the best."*

> *"Popularity is one insult I have never suffered."*

> *"The only thing worse than being talked about is not being talked about."*

> -Oscar Wilde

Oscar was born in Ireland, Oscar Fingal O'Flahertie Wills Wilde on October 16, 1854. His entire life he had a habit of lying about his age - a predilection he adopted from his Mother, who established the tradition of shaving two years off her confessed chronology.

> *"Thirty-five is an attractive age. London society is full of women of the very highest birth who have, of their own free choice, remained thirty-five for years."*

> *"No woman should ever tell her real age, it makes her look too calculating"*
>
> -Oscar Wilde

Oscar's father was a famous eye surgeon, and his mother a poet and writer from Dublin high society. As a young man, Wilde traveled to England to attend Oxford University, where he graduated with honors.

> *"There is nothing like youth. The middle aged are mortgaged to life. The old are in life's lumber-room. But youth is the Lord of life. Youth has a kingdom waiting for it. Everyone is born a king and most people die in exile, like most kings. To win back my youth . . . there is nothing I would not do, except take exercise, get up early, or be a useful member of the community."*
>
> -Oscar Wilde

Oscar broke the mold when it came to imaginative aptitude. He was the embodiment of inventive outrageousness. For Oscar Wilde, ingenious and profound statements, quotes and insights came as easily and frequently as breathing comes to the rest of us. What Oscar modeled for us is that if you do not know what creativity is . . . do not limit it! Oscar had the amazing, self-taught ability to speed-read both sides of a page simultaneously. For Wilde, reading a book appeared like he was merely paging through it. He not only read with an astonishingly high level of speed, but he also retained information with a photographic accuracy. (Wouldn't that come in handy when it comes to reading the small print on those rental car contracts.)

> *"Most people are other people. Their thoughts are some-one else's opinions, their lives a mimicry, their passions a quotation."*

> *"We teach people how to remember, we never teach them how to grow."*

> *"Life is much too important a thing ever to talk seriously about it"*
>
> -Oscar Wilde

Oscar Wilde spoke fluent English, German, French, Greek and Latin. He contributed to an 1800's movement that influenced a resurrection of the ancient Greek word aesthetes; it was in part due to Oscar's writings on this topic that we enjoy a resurgence of it today. Oscar felt that one of the fastest ways to transform the mind was to surround oneself with beauty. Wilde was a profound advocate for making and experiencing life as an art form. He was the one who encouraged the young beauty Lillie Langtry to pursue a career in the theater, thereby establishing a means of financial independence for herself.

> *"The history of woman is the history of the worst form of tyranny, of the weak over the strong. It is the only tyranny that lasts."*

"I have put only my talent into my works. I have put all my genius into my life."

"Americans know the price of everything and the value of nothing."

"I have only my genius to declare"

                                        -Oscar Wilde

The historical details of Oscar's life pale in comparison to the passion with which he lived. Where Oscar shined with the glorious light of a thousand suns, was in how he lived his life, and in his remarkable wit and clever nature. Most people have no idea that he was a deeply loving, caring and compassionate man. During the Victorian Age, the prejudice between social classes was great, but widely accepted socially. The degree to which the Victorian Age embraced this unfair yet socially approved mindset can be seen in the tragedy of the Titanic. As the Titanic was sinking, the first class passengers were given priority access to the lifeboats. Second class passengers were offered what remained after the first class had secured their preferred position on a lifeboat. Although some passengers from the steerage section did survive, many more were locked downstairs, until the wealthy and privileged could be safely removed from the doomed vessel. Imagine the lawsuits today, if a cruise liner or airline evacuated people during an emergency according to who had the most money or cultural pedigree. (Are you ready to rethink spending those frequent flier miles for that upgrade?)

"The English have a miraculous power to change wine into water."

"To disagree with three quarters of the British public on all points is one of the first elements of sanity."

"Extraordinary thing about the lower classes in England – they are always losing their relations. They are extremely fortunate in that respect."

"Work is the curse of the drinking class."

-Oscar Wilde

Oscar Wilde embodied a great Christ-like Spirituality. He refused to treat the people who worked for him as second-class citizens. He not only paid top dollar, he also insisted that the people who worked for him had access to the same food and beverages that his family enjoyed. If Oscar opened a bottle of expensive wine for his evening meal, he made sure another was opened for the people who worked for him. On holidays, those in his employ would join him and his family for the holiday meal, complete with gifts. To Oscar, everyone deserved to be treated with equal respect and dignity. This was absolutely unheard of in his time, especially for a man of his elevated social standing. When Wilde and his family went into the country on vacation, he took the people who worked for him as well, making sure they all enjoyed the same recreational benefits that his family enjoyed. A young orphaned woman who came to work for Oscar and Constance Wilde acted as a nanny to their two young boys. When the boys no longer needed a nanny, Oscar and his wife offered to adopt the young woman and send her to the college of her choice.

"Most people live for love and admiration. But it is by love and admiration that we should live."

"Anyone who lives within their means suffers from a lack of imagination."

-Oscar Wilde

Oscar Wilde is also considered to be the most tragic figure of the Victorian Age. As a result of his infamous trial he was found guilty of a charge, at the time referred to as gross indecency. In present day terms, he was found guilty of having a sexually based relationship with another man. In Oscar Wilde's time this charge came with severe consequences. The British Government seized all his assets and intellectual properties. He lost the rights to his own writings, and would never again be paid a penny for any of his resplendent literary works. The stamp of "unfit parent" came simultaneously with the conviction of gross indecency. His two young children were legally restricted from seeing him again. As a result of the social stigma attached to her husband's legal fate, his wife had to take the children, change their last name, and move to another part of Europe. Oscar himself bore the permanent mark of social pariah and outcast until his death on Nov. 1, 1900 at the age of 46. Oscar Wilde, one of the most brilliant, creative, loving, and generous souls to ever grace the planet, died homeless and penniless in a dilapidated hotel in Paris.

"Each man kills the thing he loves."

"Do not be afraid of the past. If people tell you that it is irrevocable, do not believe them. The past, the present, and the future are but one moment in the sight of God."

"Why is it that one runs to one's ruin? Why has destruction such a fascination?"

"Nothing is good in moderation. You cannot know good in anything till you have torn the heart out of it by excess."

"Always forgive your enemies; nothing annoys them so much."

"A little sincerity is a dangerous thing, and a great deal of it is absolutely fatal."

"There is no such thing as a moral or an immoral book. Books are well written or badly written. That is all."

-Oscar Wilde

When Oscar lost his trial, his friends knew that the police would descend upon his home and confiscate everything of value. It was a time of great chaos, replete with uncontrolled looting and pilfering. Original copies of Wilde's books and possessions turned up decades later all over the globe as a result of this pandemonium. Fortunately for us diehard Oscar Wilde fans, a friend of Oscar's got to the house before the others. Robert Ross managed to save some documents from Oscar's desk and library before many great treasures would either disappear or be scattered to the winds of time. In the surviving papers was a thank you letter to Oscar, from a family unknown to him. Wilde, it seems, was having lunch at one of his favorite restaurants. He overheard a banker dining near by, talking about an overdue mortgage, and how unlucky it was for this family that was about to lose their ancestral home. Oscar found out how much the debt was and paid it anonymously. Through the banker, the family determined who it was, and sent Oscar a letter expressing their gratitude. Descriptive of his values is another story of Wilde. While walking with a friend one evening, they were held up at knifepoint. When Oscar realized the man robbing them had little or no clothes on under his shabby cloak, Oscar not only gave the man all his money, he took off his own cloak and lovingly wrapped it around the thief! It takes a Wilde Spiritual devotion of unconditional love to show up on the planet Earth, as a force of

Love that cannot be robbed, because Oscar Wilde would give you what you needed, and Bless you in the process.

"The false and the true are merely forms of intellectual existence."

"I can resist anything but temptation."

"Experience is the name everyone gives to their mistakes."

-Oscar Wilde

Oscar's last days were spent in a rundown hotel in Paris. (Definitely no Hilton Honors points at this place.) The owner of the hotel gave Oscar the room to die in. It is suspected that the hotel owner could not read, and therefore had no recognition of Wilde as a brilliant writer. The hotel owner knew Oscar as a local homeless man. However he considered Oscar a Saint, because he saw him love and share whatever he had with the all the other homeless people. Even in his last moments Oscar is Wildely Spiritual. As he was dying, Oscar showed up as a force of Love, wit, wisdom and humor, in a whole life tragedy that would leave most people angry and bitter.

"No man is rich enough to buy back his past."

"I did not know it was such a pain to die: I though that life had taken all the agonies to itself."

"I cannot even afford to die. I am dying beyond my means."

And finally, Oscar Wilde's last words, *"The wallpaper and I are fighting a duel to the death. Either the wallpaper goes or I do."*

Long live the miraculous force of Divine Love we know as Oscar Wilde!

"We are all in the gutter, but some of us are looking at the stars."

– Oscar Wilde

The Bodhisattva of the Bijou

You never forget your first love. The power of that exquisite experience leaves an indelible impression upon the heart, psyche and perspective. Once you have embraced your first love into your life, he or she remains forever a part of your existence. If you are very, very fortunate, you find a rare jewel for a first love as I did. A once in a life time, or maybe a once in two or three lifetimes, precious con-nection that all other intimacies in your life become destined to be measured by. Looking back on it now I see the traces of my first love's influences running rampant throughout my life, like footprints in the sand along the beach; while no real person can be seen there, the evidence of their presence is indisputable.

It was the summer of my thirteenth birthday, that magical time when the awakening of adulthood is stirring, and yet one still carries that pure innocence, openness and receptivity that is the supreme power of childhood. I met my first love within the pages of a book. Not just any book, mind you; it was a love letter of a book, so profound it impacted me like an inner revolution forever coloring how I viewed the world. My first love is film director Frank Capra. The book, his autobiography "The Name Above The Title." It heralded a demarcation point in my life. That day forward became AF, after Frank, and the time before noted as BF, before Frank.

Our relationship started the way most authentic love stories start. He gently took my hand and walked me through a remarkable journey. Frank withheld nothing from his partner, a full and utterly beautiful action of complete disclosure. A gifted storyteller, he punctuated his sharing with humor, a lifetime of hard won wisdom, and heart breaking honesty. By virtue of his love, he bequeathed me a depth of character and resilience that no mere teenager could embody without Divine intervention. But Frank was no novice at this mastery of touching and painting upon another's soul. He had spent a lifetime refining and perfecting this mind altering, if not life altering, Capra-esque communication.

Regardless of what age you are when you learn of Frank's life, the sheer enormity of hard work and tenacity he applied to grow beyond his immigrant, impoverished beginnings is humbling. His family resented his unwillingness to abandon his education; he refused to crumble beneath the pressure that he must play his role as just another "slave laborer", never destined for anything more than a life revolving around survival at its most basic level. Frank fought for his street smarts, his desire to require more from life, his fearlessness to express and value himself outside of family controlling and culturally myopic thinking.

The most endearing aspect of Frank's love is his ability to celebrate the Divinity of the single individual: his unmistakable talent for perceiving the Divine as alive and well within the average human being, inextinguishable and indestructible against the onslaught of all of life's suffering, pain and gut-wrenching disappointments. You can see this quality quite clearly in his films. Every character, even the smallest role, is hypnotically rich, multi-dimensional. They radiate an otherworldly embodiment of power, even in their deepest experiences of vulnerability and their weakest, most fragile moments. Frank reflects the full spectrum of what it means to be human. He captures the essence of it like a finely crafted ring setting enhances a priceless diamond. How could one not surrender to his love? He imbues his films with a voice that is as intoxicating as the sirens that called to Ulysses.

The most challenging aspect of any Spiritual teaching is to convey the sacredness of accepting and allowing oneself to be tempered by the whole of the human experience. It is easy when things are going our way to embrace life and permit it to touch, mold and shape our existence. It requires a completely different mindset and inner discipline to remain open and mutable to forces we instinctually resist and contract from. To compose oneself and remain as present for an agonizing, emotionally debilitating moment as we do for a highly glamorous and rewarding one, is the difference between a Spiritually awakened, mature being and an unenlightened, Spiritually undeveloped being.

Frank taught me so much about how to refine and surrender to this gift for appreciating unconditionally the whole of life that is the basis of all great Spiritual teachings. Frank did not censor himself in the living of his own life or in writing about it. His remarkably candid book reflects the care and meticulous consideration he gave to the whole of his own life.

Frank was the first filmmaker to corner the top four honors at the Academy Awards. In 1934 his film *It Happened One Night*, a classic romantic comedy, was the first to win best picture, best director, best actress (Claudette Colbert), and best actor (Clark Gable). This was Gable's only Academy Award by the way.

Frank allowed that experience to wash over him in the same way Super Bowl winners allow free flowing champagne to baptize them in glory. After his golden day in the sun with *It Happened One Night,* Frank talked about the nagging, unshakeable fear of failure that began to take over his mind. The burden of how he would ever be able to keep up with his own success became a crippling obstacle, paralyzing his creativity and movement forward. Gradually it completely consumed his life like a slow-moving, emotional cancer.

When sharing his story, Frank did not shrink away from this part of the evolution of his soul. Like any other sage master who has learned to be neutral in the labeling of things as good or bad, Frank illuminated, with the same attention to detail, his descent into a self-made hell of panic attacks and non-stop stomach churning nausea, as he had about the moment he first put his hands on the coveted, golden Oscar. Frank ended up in the hospital, fully expecting to die. His fears about the future sucked the life right out of his present moment and his body. A visitor suddenly appeared; a man he had never met before or seen since. Frank referred to him as "as faceless a man as you will ever see". The visitor told Frank that he had the gift of being able talk to millions of people for two hours in the dark, and he had no right to abandon that gift for a fixation on fear. This man shocked Frank into acknowledging he had a responsibility to Divine Love and Wisdom, and he could not fulfill it lying in that bed. Frank understood this faceless man was his wake-up call, his reminder that life is not a goal oriented event; it is a journey. And how fully you show up for that journey is what is of critical importance. It is the very meaning and purpose of life itself. Frank realized he had set into motion this illness that was causing his life to swirl down the drain, and that now he alone was accountable for his recovery.

That recovery took the several years between *It Happened One Night* and Frank's next film *Mr. Deeds Goes To Town*, for which he won his second Academy Award. But what Frank's ordeal taught me has lasted my entire life. Every time I sense the insidious grip of the "what if I fail" fear attempting to creep into my life, I think about Frank pulling himself out of that hospital bed, barely alive and willing himself back to life. I decided that thirteenth summer of my life, while reading Frank's love letter book, that I was going to get out of that hospital bed with him. If Frank wasn't going down, then neither was I. You can see the magnificent spectrum of growth Frank made in those two years when you watch *Mr. Deeds Goes To Town*. Our protagonist, exquisitely played by Gary Cooper, is a small town man who inherits $20 million. He moves to New York and has full-time work protecting himself from virtually everyone, including his friends, who are working hard to separate him from his money. His small town naivety is replaced by cynicism as self-preservation wears on him. His desire to help less fortunate farmers coupled with his own unscrupulous lawyers finally break him, emotionally and perceptually, resulting in his connecting more fully and authentically to the potential of his life and relationships. Mr. Deeds gets the whole of life and has to find his own way through that darkness to the Light. He struggles with a world that both richly blesses him and simultaneously threatens to destroy him. Mr. Deeds learns to value vulnerability as another form of wealth. In so doing, he transforms and uplifts everyone around him.

Frank is the undisputed master at creating a body of work that accurately traces the painstaking and exhaustive nuances involved in systemic personal transformation. In *Mr. Smith Goes To Washington*, Mr. Smith, played by James Stewart, is introduced as idealistic, innocent of corruption, and prone to wildly romanticize the world around him. Isn't this the way we all are when we first begin to imagine the potential of our lives, when we are young and inexperienced in the ways of the world? Mr. Smith's journey to Washington D.C. as a junior Senator changes this naivety. He is mercilessly welcomed to the "real" world of emotional, psychological and experiential maturity. His dreams are disemboweled, his ideals are crushed, and his view of the world melts like an ice cream on a hot day. Frank captures every subtle, flinching, inner response of this political neophyte. Like the phoenix, Mr. Smith has to be burned to ashes and leveled by life's brutalities, before he can rise up. It is exactly this type of journey into hell that gives us the wisdom to know how to find our way into Heaven. Mr. Smith is no different than us. Everyone has to experience the whole of life.

Frank brings this astounding force of the tempering of the human soul to cinematic life. It is the triumph of the Divine within each individual that ultimately emerges in self-resurrection a la Capra. Through the instrument of film making, Frank, like an Eastern Indian coaxing the cobra from a basket, brings out the inner Mr. Smith and Dr. Deeds within each of us.

To this day I cannot hear a train whistle, boat anchor chain, or airplane engine without feeling connected to George Bailey from *It's A Wonderful Life,* best known as the classic Christmas movie. He longed to travel the world and journey to far off exotic places. But due to life circumstances and obligations, poor George never managed to shake the dust of his little hometown from his shoes. When George is faced with imminent financial ruin and possible jail time, he wishes that he had never been born. Who, while struggling with their greatest, most crushing life challenges, cannot connect with those feelings? George is sent his slightly awkward but genuinely lovable guardian Angel, Clarence, who shows him what the world would be like if he had never been born. For George, as it is for the viewer, the evidence of one missing life, no matter how small and insignificant that life appears, impacts the world dramatically. It makes a life-size, irreplaceable hole. That is the heart of Frank's movie mojo: each person's life is extraordinarily powerful, beyond measure. We are here for a purpose, and without us, the world would not be the same; it *would* miss us. Each of us is Divinely designed to be here, to interact and to be a part of the greater whole. The Divine design is not complete without each of us. Frank once again has his fingers directly on the pulse of the mystical Universal "every person" within each of us. He accomplished this in every film - flawlessly. Not a casual or accidental feat.

In *Pocketful Of Miracles*, Frank stretches character growth to a new level of multi-dimensional flexibility. Bette Davis plays Apple Annie, a skid row beggar woman who sells apples on the street by day and guzzles cheap gin to drown her personal sorrows at night. Annie sells her apples to a local gangster, played by Glenn Ford, who superstitiously feels Annie's apples bring him invincible luck. Our self-absorbed, shallow, emotionally bankrupt gangster, by virtue of his "need" for Annie's apples, ends up helping her transform into a high society lady. Nearly twenty years previously, Annie had sent her only daughter, shortly after her birth, to Europe to be raised by Nuns. Now her freshly engaged, grown daughter (played by Ann Margaret in her film debut) is coming from Europe for a first-time visit to her mother, Annie, with her betrothed and prestigious "family to be" in tow. Annie has been writing, pretending to be of wealth and of a high social caliber, and now is devastated by the reality she may be exposed and ruin her daughter's chances at a successful life. Frank takes both of these characters to a place where, against all odds, they must expand their perceptions of themselves. Forced to grow in ways they never imagined possible, these characters must now stretch to accommodate this greater, more profound state of development. Then like a rubber band, he snaps them back into their comfort zone of limitation and defensiveness. This process of growing then retreating back into fear is a repeating theme in the film. Frank uses these same dynamic forces of expansion and contraction that life throws at us all, to exorcise his film characters of their inner demons and most tenacious fears.

Consistent with Frank's other productions, every single character, regardless of how big their role, is an absolute star in their own right. Every character is a beacon reflecting the sacredness of the single individual and the precious Divinity of the human soul. Peter Falk, comically, yet convincingly, portrays Glenn Ford's right hand man. He is a scene-stealer in every frame. Falk watches the monumental changes happening within everyone around him, while taking great pride in his own immunity to the nonsense and no-profit status of self-improvement. The examination of the human experience in Frank Capra films is complete in every aspect.

In my thirteen-year-old love-struck state, I wrote Frank a letter confessing my intoxicated devotion to his brilliance and relentless commitment to empower the ordinary, average person with the glorious recognition they deserve as the Divine forces of love they truly are. I wrote the letter not expecting to hear back. I wrote the letter because Frank confessed in his book the feelings of worthlessness he wrestled with in his retirement. I felt the man needed to be set straight, and that I was just the right know-it-all teenager for the job. I did feel greatly relieved after writing and mailing the letter. I somehow knew that Frank would get the message that he had made a profound and meaningful difference in the world; that he must never overlook that. Frank was simply too precious to ever let that happen. And as my first love, I was not going to allow it. That was all there was to it!

Many months passed since I mailed my Capra manifesto. Frank was and always would be an integral part of me. Frank could not be closer to me if he was in my very DNA. One day I came home from school through the side door that took me through the laundry room. The daily routine upon arriving home from school started with collecting the clean and neatly folded laundry, taking it upstairs and putting it away. If my other siblings or I ever got any mail, it was always placed on top of the individually stacked laundry pile for pick-up.

I remember very clearly seeing the small handwritten envelope gingerly placed on my clothes like a flag planted on a mountain peak. My hands started to shake as I recognized the return address. It was from Frank! My beloved Frank had written me back! Oh, most immortal of moments, my most treasured of all memories.

As I stepped out of the laundry room, I noticed my mother and father sitting anxiously at the kitchen table. My mother had called my father when she recognized the return address, and he rushed home from work to witness this sacred occasion. I sat down in the chair next to them, barely able to open the letter. My excitement was so great it was nearly paralyzing. My parents were as eager to hear the contents as I was. They began to chant like a Greek chorus, "What does it say? What does it say?" The words and feelings expressed in Frank's letter were so beautiful, so loving, I could not speak. The warm flash of uncontrollable tears blinded my vision and choked my throat. My father reached over and took the letter from me. Now with only a Greek chorus of one, my mother continued chanting, "What does it says? What does it say?" My father started crying too, before he could externalize what he was reading. My mother reached over and took the letter from him and began silently reading. Soon, all three of us were sitting around the table overcome with emotion and tears.

Frank wrote that if he was King of the world, and he had all the gold, all the jewels, and everything precious and valuable in the world, it would not mean as much to him as the knowledge that he had touched one little girl's heart. Now how can anyone compare to such a love as this?

When I was in my senior year in high school, I took an extension class from a local university on the films of Frank Capra. The professor told the class that he had written Frank, and that Frank had agreed to come speak to the class. Oh, holy of holies, could it be? Would I finally be able to personalize this great love affair? I counted the days, the minutes, the seconds that would finally unite my beloved and I in the same room. I arrived over an hour early for class, staking out the most prized real estate: a seat in the front row. When the professor arrived conspicuously bereft of Frank's presence, I knew in my bones my letter was the closest I was ever going to get to actually sharing time with Frank.

The professor explained that Frank was not feeling well and would not be able to attend the class as originally planned. Everyone else in the class went on with life. By the next week they would have completely forgotten that Frank never showed. But now, over three decades later, I still feel a profound loss at that missed opportunity.

One September day, years later while attending college, I kept getting the overwhelming feeling that Frank had crossed over – I felt persistently revisited by the feeling that many close friends were wishing me well, because they had heard that Frank had died. When I got home, I no sooner walked through the front door than I received a phone call from a concerned friend who said, "I just kept thinking about you all day when I heard Frank died."

The truth is, Love never dies. The body falls away, but Love never dies. Frank will always be as close to me as my heartbeat. The kind of magic Frank created is immortal and eternal. As long as there is a Heaven, there will always be a theatre showing a Frank Capra movie. *That* is what makes it Heaven!

Stand-up Spiritual Teachers

*B*eing a Spiritual teacher is like any other calling. All kinds of people with unlikely backgrounds and talents find themselves occupying that role. Two of my favorite Spiritual teachers are best known for their day jobs, actually their night jobs, or should I say their nightclub work. Lenny Bruce and Bill Hicks both knew they were serving a greater purpose than merely transforming stand-up comedy into a revolutionary commentary and new way of perceiving reality. They knew they were Spiritual teachers, and they were both forthcoming about stating that fact. Lenny and Bill both firmly took their stand among the ranks of those who dared to speak the Truth in the face of popular opinion and in direct opposition to a mob mentality of ignorance.

> *"Every day people are straying away from the church and going back to God."*
>
> – Lenny Bruce

Lenny Bruce died in August 1968, long before Bill Hicks, armed only with a sense of humor and the naked Truth, took center stage in the single spotlight. But without Lenny, Bill would have inherited an entirely different world of comedy. As Lenny put it, *"Today's comedian has a cross to bear that he built himself. A comedian of the older generation did an "act" and he told the audience, 'This is my act.'"* It was all cheap one-liners like, "Take my wife, please!" and cheesy impressions like James Cagney saying, "You dirty rat." In Lenny's own words, *"Today's comic is not doing an act. The audience assumes he's telling the truth. What is truth today may be a damn lie next week."*

> *"The only honest art form is laughter, comedy. You can't fake it . . . try to fake three laughs in an hour - ha ha ha ha ha - they'll take you away, man. You can't"*
>
> – Lenny Bruce

Lenny transformed stand-up comedy into the in-depth examination of America's cultural hypocrisies, perverted social value system and honest exploration of our fears and biases. Thanks to Lenny, this would be a typical stand-up routine in a present day comedy club. He perfected the fine art of making comedy a viable vehicle for socially redeeming commentary. Around the same time, there were others emerging that were also pushing the envelope: Mort Sahl, Dick Gregory, Shelly Berman and Steve Allen. However, Lenny pushed the boundaries of social limitations harder, deeper, and faster than anyone one else, and trust me, Lenny would have loved this porno language pun.

> *"The liberals can understand everything but the people who don't understand them."*
>
> – Lenny Bruce

Lenny was the first comic to be arrested for indecent language. Language that is still edgy by today's standards. But next to comics like George Carlin, Richard Pryor, Chris Rock, and Andrew Dice Clay, Lenny looks like an altar boy, or the Jewish equivalent. Most comics, post Lenny, have used "colorful" words merely for the shock value. Lenny was extremely deliberate in his use of words as a means of directing attention to taboo areas. Lenny was referred to as the "sick comic" of his day, when the truth of the matter is, all that Lenny was guilty of was exposing where we, as a society, are inwardly and perceptually ill. He started one of his acts by asking, *"By the way, are there any niggers here tonight? What did he say! Is he that desperate for shock value? I think I see one nigger couple back there between those two niggers to three kikes. Thank God for the kikes . . . and two spiks and one mick . . . The point is, if President Kennedy got on television every day and said, 'I would like to introduce all the niggers in my cabinet,' and every day you heard nigger, nigger, nigger, in the second month, nigger wouldn't mean as much as goodnight."* Lenny knew that the word would lose its negative charge.

> *"A lot of people ask me, 'Why did you kill Christ?' I dunno, it was that kind of party, things just got out of hand, you know."*
>
> – Lenny Bruce

Lenny paid the price for being so far ahead of his time. After numerous arrests, between the court fees and the lawyers to defend his right to free speech, Lenny was slowly bled financially and creatively dry. The constant police harassment and unending legal entanglements emotionally and psychologically crushed him. In 1964 a New York jury found Lenny guilty of obscenity - his only guilty conviction. But it did not matter; the pressure had already taken its toll. On December 23, 2003, Lenny became the only person to have his conviction posthumously overturned. I celebrated this pardon as an indication that we as a nation, as a people, almost 40 years later might have finally caught up to Lenny Bruce, the man who dared reveal our flaws, our obsession with shallowness and pretense of morality. Lenny, the man who was thrown under the First Amendment bus so that we would not have to take accountability for our own insecurities and neuroses, was finally free of the dirty stigma of our collectively diseased judgment.

"In the Halls of Justice the only justice is in the halls."

– Lenny Bruce

Like all good Spiritual teachers, Lenny got right up in our faces, forcing us to look at our own self-created bad faith and self-imposed limitations. Eastern Spiritual traditions encourage us to look at the charges that we have created with our own minds, with our own perceptions. Then they urge us to end the bondage that we alone have put into motion. We created the charges; only we can resolve these charges. Lenny is the greatest American Spiritual teacher of this tradition. He exposed the charges that we have projected onto words and then, with humor and wit, implored us to end that tyranny. Lenny observed that the word "elbow" is not any dirtier than the word "toilet," and if we are experiencing a difference between those words, we are accountable for that charge, because we alone created it.

"The only truly anonymous donor is the guy who knocks up your daughter."

– Lenny Bruce

If we brought together five people who never heard the English language before, asked them to listen to a litany of words, some being explicative in nature and others being socially benign, those listening would not know the difference. Words, in and of themselves, are not intrinsically good or bad. Words are neutral. There is no force within words that can jump out and rape our minds. We put that energy into place. We decide within the privacy of our own minds, with our own free will, what is good and what is bad. We created that distinction and then gave it power. That means that only we can destroy that power. We all have free will, so no one person can control the words other people use. Instead of attempting to control and conform the verbal expressions of others, instead of being hurt and offended by the words other people choose to use, it would be wiser to free our minds from the tyranny of words altogether. Although comedy may have caught up to Lenny in this respect, the fact that people still lose their jobs over the "n-word" highlights our still unresolved sensitivity. Jesse Jackson referring to New York City as "Hymie Town" may have offended many people, but I can assure you that Lenny would have howled with laughter if he had lived to hear it.

> *"I dedicate this book to all the followers of Christ and his teachings; in particular to a true Christian, Jimmy Hoffa – because he hired ex-convicts as, I assume, Christ would have."*
>
> – Lenny Bruce,
> "How To Talk Dirty And Influence People"

We created this linguistic battlefield; we can also create an ending to it. It is impossible to manipulate the world to the degree that it will finally fit everyone's agenda of what is good and perfect. Controlling the world or other people has never been the answer. Letting the world be, while we liberate our inner life from the self-created charges that hold us hostage, always has been and always will be the ultimate solution.

"The 'what should be' never did exist, but people keep trying to live up to it. There is no 'what should be,' there is only what is."

— Lenny Bruce

Lenny excelled as an innovator of social redeeming Spiritual philosophies cleverly camouflaged as stand-up comedy. But growing beyond the limitation of language was not the only topic he scrutinized. Lenny struck a raw nerve in his audience whenever he talked about sex. What clearly confused Lenny about our cultural prudishness was why people were so fundamentally inflamed over the expression of love, caring and tenderness between two consenting adults. Lenny observed that we are collectively much more comfortable with accepting the presence of physical violence than we are with the act of pro-creation which, by the way, is how we continue the human race. Lenny pointed out that parents are much more open to allowing their children to watch television or movies with violence in them, than they are with letting their children see two people openly sharing affection for one another. What does it say about a culture that tolerates graphic physical violence as a legitimate form of entertainment, while labeling life-affirming intimacy as "sick" and "ugly"? Nobody is arguing that there is an appropriate time, place and method for educating children on adult matters, but when you really look at the level of blood-soaked, body dismembering, alien organ eating violence the average child witnesses as entertainment, how can we get upset by the site of two people holding hands and kissing?

"There are never enough I Love You's."

— Lenny Bruce

Every comic who came after Lenny, and certainly Bill Hicks, was in a much improved, more protected place to speak their brand of Truth and humor. That was a very good thing. Bill Hicks came like a bolt of lightening to illuminate the world with his unique quality of wit and wisdom. For Bill Hicks, the only thing that was sacred was that nothing was sacred. There were no limits. He was an equal opportunity "amusement engineer" as he called himself. Bill had more than just a little something to say about every aspect of the human experience; no topic was beyond Bill's comic expertise. Politics was one of Bill's favorite subjects, whether it was politicians themselves or a politically hot topic such as abortion. Bill's stand on that issue was, *"If you're so pro-life, do me a favor. Don't lock arms and block medical clinics. If you're so pro-life, lock arms and block cemeteries. Let's see how committed you are to this f*cking premise."*

Bill took on religious beliefs as well. Bill said he was once cornered in a parking lot by a group of angry men that informed him that they were "good Christians", and they did not like what Bill had been saying on stage. Bill's response was to look them fearlessly in the eye and say, *"Then forgive me."* Bill never apologized for his comic opinion. He stood his ground in what could have turned into an ugly incident and informed this group that if they were truly good Christians, then do what Jesus would do: forgive him and move on with their lives. Like any good Spiritual teacher, he knew how to make people aware of their hypocrisies.

"Women priests. Great, great. Now there's priests of both sexes I don't listen to."

— Bill Hicks

Bill loved to tread on everything "sacred" in our society. Like Lenny Bruce, he found a voice inviting us to examine life and the world from a broader perspective and a more honest filter. Bill did not shy away from unpopular points of view, no matter how socially counter-culture the point might be. He could not understand why the media's perspective on drug stories was always negative.

> *"How about a positive LSD story. Wouldn't that be newsworthy just once to base your story on information rather than scare tactics and superstitions and lies? Just once, I think it would be news worthy. 'Today a young man on acid realized that all matter is merely energy condensed to a slow vibration; that we are all one consciousness experiencing itself subjectively. There is no such thing as death. Life is only a dream, and we are the imagination of ourselves . . . here's Tom with the weather'. . . ."*
>
> – Bill Hicks

Bill Hicks, the Spiritual teacher, offers us the opportunity to examine consciousness itself and the nature of ultimate reality. Not exactly your standard stand-up comic fare. He understood that laughter is a therapeutic method of addressing "what is" from a less self-defensive vantage point. Bill's value system was that of a classic Spiritual teacher as well. Sharing his ideas on the purpose of life he commented, *"As long as one person lives in darkness then it seems to be a responsibility to tell other people. And if I can take part in it by transforming my own consciousness, then someone else's, I'm happy to do it."*

All the great Eastern Spiritual philosophies talk about life on

Earth as an "illusion." This is a notion that is very difficult for most Western minds to fully understand, because we have a tendency to think of "illusion" as meaning a trick, sleight of hand, or smoke and mirrors. This is not what these philosophies meant. A better way to interpret the use of this word would be to understand that life here on Earth is not what we think and believe it is. More than that, what we think and believe is actually a detriment, a distraction that prohibits deeper more profound states of self-realization. What we think and believe about ourselves, our true nature, our relationships, is an illness we have come here to grow beyond. Bill understood this sage inner wisdom. He expressed that knowledge brilliantly in a piece he would introduce as the entire point of his act:

> *"The world is like a ride at an amusement park and
> when you choose to go on it, you think it's real, because
> that is how powerful our minds are. And the ride goes
> up and down, and round and round, and it has thrills
> and chills, and it is very brightly colored, and it is very
> loud. And it is fun for a while. Some people have been
> on it for a very long time, and they begin to question, 'Is
> this real, or is it just a ride?' And other people have re-
> membered, and they have come back to us, and they say,
> 'Hey, don't worry, don't be afraid, ever . . . because this
> is just a ride'. . . and we kill those people. 'Shut him, up!
> We have a lot invested in this ride; shut him up! Look at
> my furrow of worry, look at my big bank account, and
> my family . . . this just has to be real.'*

> *It's just a ride. But we always try to kill those good guys
> who try to tell us that. You ever notice that? And let the
> demons run amok. But it does not matter, because it's
> just a ride, and we can change it any time we want. It's*

only a choice. No effort, no work, no job, no savings of money, a choice right now, between fear and love. The eyes of fear want you to put bigger locks on your door, buy guns, close yourself off. The eyes of love instead see all of us as One. Here's what we can do to change the world right now to a better ride. Take all that money we spend on weapons and defense each year and instead spend it on feeding, clothing and educating the poor of the world, which it would many times over, not one human excluded. And we could explore space together both inner and outer forever in peace."

– Bill Hicks

Bill died on February 26, 1994 of pancreatic cancer. Like all authentic Spiritual teachers, Bill did not recognize a personal death; he clearly knew he would be back to get on "the ride" again, because exploring the true nature of consciousness is eternal and unending. And it is the only thing that's real.

"I left in love, in laughter, and in truth, and wherever truth, love and laughter abide, I am there in spirit."

– Bill Hicks

Maybe we didn't agree with what they said or the way they said it, but Lenny Bruce and Bill Hicks made us question our paradigm. They challenged the current belief system of our culture, making us doubt our own perspective on issues and situations in an in-your-face, irreverent, and sometimes offensive style. They made all of us look a little deeper, and that is a good thing. But that shouldn't come as surprise. After all, they were really Spiritual teachers masquerading through life as comics.

St. Lenny . . . died for our sins."

– Eric Bogosian, introduction to
"How to Talk Dirty and Influence People"

The "H" Word

Happiness. It is something we all want. The constitution of the United States ensures our protected right to pursue it. But what exactly is it? Someone once told me they found happiness. Gee, I didn't even know it was lost. Is happiness attainable by discovery? Is it at a geographic location? I know you can get 2 tickets to paradise, but I haven't seen Travelocity booking vacations to the happiness destination . . . at least not as an Internet special. Maybe it is a state. Yes, people often desire to live in a state of happiness. But no one seems to permanently reside there. Sounds a lot like Florida, but I know it is not one of the 50. So maybe it's more like Guam or Puerto Rico. I sure hope it's got a tropical climate, complete with frou-frou drinks adorned with cute colorful little umbrellas. Oh, and no income tax. It can't have income tax.

Maybe as so many imply happiness can be bought. The Beatles tell us, "Money can't buy me love." But they don't mention the H word. Hmm, so maybe you can buy happiness. I looked in Walmart; I checked out Urban Outfitters; I even went through the Victoria's Secret Catalog. No go. Maybe I should just ask Paris Hilton. If you could shop for happiness, she would know not only where to find it, but also the price, size, and availability. So how come she doesn't behave like the happiest person alive? Apparently shopping promotes happiness, but only for a short period of time. Looks like we need to keep on searching.

Aha! It's a pharmaceutical. Nope, that's ecstasy. And in the "other" drug world, the H word is already taken by heroin. Of course that happiness has a pretty short shelf life and an extremely expensive price tag ~ your soul. But like shopping, it does seem to make some people happy, at least until the high wears off.

Hmm, *make* someone happy? Isn't that forcing something on someone? Babies are happy; no one seems to be forcing anything on them. They just simply appear to embody happiness.

I hate to admit it, but I think we failed. We still haven't ascertained what happiness is. If we don't know what it is, maybe we should see what it isn't. Happiness is not what you *think* it is. No. Literally, happiness is not a mental function; it is not what you *think*. You'd think that the smarter (or richer) a person is, the happier they'd be. It actually looks like the opposite is true. People who experience severe forms of mental developmental challenges are mostly happy, playful, and in the present moment. Proof positive that what you *think* will not insure happiness. If intellectual prowess equated to happiness, then every rocket scientist and brain surgeon would be deliriously ecstatic. And it would follow that the greater one excelled in the mental *thought* process, the happier one became. The world's eggheads would be known Universally for their mirth and happy-go-lucky contagious personalities… clearly not the case. Their reputation for being in desperate need of a fashion consultant and void of any animated engagement with life precedes them.

Thinking has nothing to do with happiness. You can be thinking about how you have to lose weight, pick up dog pooh in the back yard, organize your tax records and still be happy! Impossible you say? Not really. Vedic psychology says that happiness and enlightenment have something in common: being in the present moment with an open heart, and not having a problem with it. Being with "what is" and not judging it, not resisting it, but being with it - one with an open-hearted perspective, not an *intellectual* posturing.

Let's go back for a moment to people who are severely challenged due to mental developmental issues. A friend was recently sharing with me about his daughter who is sixteen. At the time of her birth, doctors told him that she would not live very long. A severe medical complication would not allow her to develop any mental capacity beyond that of a three or four month old baby. My friend is always telling me about how incredibly happy his daughter is ~ always smiling, laughing, just in the moment. She never projects off into the future or gets stuck in a past event, unable to experience the present moment freely. She never has an attachment to any outcome. She does not experience life through the "should have," "could have," "would have," or "better have" filter. My friend tells me that without his daughter, he would never have seen the face of genuine happiness. She is the ultimate happiness teacher, unconditional in her relationship with it.

Does what we give our attention to affect our emotions? Absolutely! That is clear and self-evident to anyone with a nervous system. Anyone who has ever spent more than five minutes worrying about anything can vouch for that. So how can one be giving their attention to the reality that they need to lose weight, pick up Rover's aromatic calling card in the back yard, organize their tax records, and still be happy? If you are aware of all these things *while being in the present moment with an open heart,* you have discovered the pivotal element.

When in the present moment with an open heart, you are accepting of the place you presently find yourself standing. There is no judgment, no flogging or rejection of yourself for how you got there, merely an acceptance of "what is" that frees you to now respond to what is in your best interest. "Okay, it would serve me to lose a few pounds. I can do that. I got myself here, I can get myself to where I need to be." No whining, no gnashing of teeth, or screaming banshee cries of the pain that originates from denying oneself the joy of empty calories; simply accepting "what is" in one's own best interest, because there is no other agenda or dysfunctional focus.

Yeah, but what about Rover's perennial "love offering"? Another friend of mine was sharing with me her daily ritual of retrieving Duke's recycled food products. She was telling me that since her father's death, every time she scoured the backyard for canine deposited land mines, she dropped into her heart and thanked God that Duke, her beloved golden retriever, was alive and healthy. Clearly she was not suffering from doo-doo denial. She was giving her attention to getting the job done, but it was happening from a heart-felt place grounded in the present moment.

I was in a car accident, and it took me nearly a decade to fully recover. For years I could not work, make money, or think as clearly as I had before. Now, every time I sit down to organize my tax records, I am just happy to be working again. I am thrilled to be able to carry out simple tasks without anguishing frustration. I am grateful beyond measure to be able to make enough income that I have to now file a 1040 Form. What I have learned from my friends, and from my own life, is that happiness can be unconditional.

If happiness seems a rare or foreign event in your life now, it is simply because being in the present moment and not having a problem with it, is not the attitude you have practiced most often. Consider how much of your attention is consumed with worrying about bills, what body parts are sagging, what tattooed, body-pierced prize your teenager will be dating next. Imagine how different your life would feel if you practiced not having a problem with the present moment to the same degree that you have practiced blaming the present moment for delivering something that you are dissatisfied with.

Clearly there is a connection with having a problem with the present moment and being tense, angry, anxious, depressed, and lonely. Even though having a problem with the present moment has never solved a single problem or improved the quality of our lives, it is perversely ironic how we cling to the practice of it. We stubbornly hold a grudge, not releasing it under any circumstances.

Vedic psychology says that it is the ego part of our consciousness that literally "hates" the present moment, because it sees the present moment through this blaming filter. Every time you find yourself projecting off into the future or reliving something from the past, you are experiencing the ego's subtle hatred for the present moment, by distracting your awareness away from it. Enlightenment, the process of freeing our minds from any limitation, does not happen in the past or the future; it happens in the present moment. That is why it is essential to practice being here now.

The added perk to being in the present moment with an open heart is that the tyranny of the ego loses its power in that state.

The ego needs some source of unhappiness in order maintain its hold over the human mind. The ego likes to be the master of our lives, pushing us around emotionally. The ego strives to makes us the servant, training us to serve it by constantly surrendering our attention to things in the present moment that we can find fault with. When we practice accepting the present moment as it is, we are in actuality cutting the ego off from its biggest food source, and forcing it back into the servant role it is designed to have.

What if we had nothing to lose but our relationship with and perpetuation of unhappiness; if we released the death grip we have on finding fault with the present moment? What if we chose to practice being deeply and profoundly loyal to an infinitely more life-sustaining attitude? What if a more meaningful, enjoyable and healthier existence could be obtained by simply choosing to relate to this moment with an open heart, instead of a toxic opinion?

There is an old saying that the longest journey one will ever make is the eighteen inches from the frontal lobe down into the heart. If you can find your way out of your head and into your heart in this moment, you too will find that happiness has been waiting there for you all along. And by the way, "welcome home!"

Section 3 ~ Spirituality

You Are What You Love

You are what you love, and you love whatever you are giving your attention to. Eastern Spiritual psychologies profess that whatever you give your attention to, is what you are making your God. If, for example, you spend all your time thinking about that next cigarette, then you have just made that next nicotine fix your God. If you are worrying about your bills, your daughter's boyfriend with the spiked hair and nose ring, the price of oil, the likelihood of another terrorist attack or CNN's reported "fear du jour", then you love worrying and stressing out about your life. Surprising isn't it?! Not really, because we in the West consider love to be associated with something we have a positive affection for. However, according to the Eastern sciences of self-healing, love is where your attention goes, regardless of whether or not it is for something ultimately life enhancing. Really makes you want to clean up where your attention goes, doesn't it?

The link between love and attention is synonymous, because of the Eastern definition of our Spiritual nature. Spirit *is* awareness itself. Spirit is inseparable from awareness, consciousness, or any other buzzword you'd like to use for it. Consciousness is what we bring with us when we come to the Earth plane. It is also what we take with us when the body expires and we shed the mortal coil. Awareness *is* our Divinity, our God juice so to speak. Therefore whatever we give our attention to, we are empowering with life-giving energy. Suddenly the value of being more discriminate with our attention seems like a Spiritually mature and Enlightened thing to do.

Emanuel Swedenborg offers great practical advice when it comes to how to manage our awareness in our every day lives. Swedenborg suggested that we only give our attention to what lives in Heaven. For the sake of this sharing, we are going to define Heaven as a place of existence, or state of being, that is unlimited, and hell as the opposite. Swedenborg says when you find yourself giving attention to some thing outside of Heaven, simply stop, put it down and return your attention to Prime Source. Brings a whole new meaning to keeping your "eye on the prize". Swedenborg goes on further to explain that we have to *live* according to our love. If you love what lives in Heaven then you will become a good resident of Heaven; if you love what lives in hell, then that will become your mailing address, and that is where you will find yourself living. Seems that is enough right there to inspire an attention ascension.

Swedenborg started out as a great scientist. As such, he'd rather we prove this shared wisdom to ourselves than take his word for it. When we as Spirit adopt a physical body, it comes complete with a nervous system. Swedenborg says that the purpose of this sensory feedback mechanism is that it keeps us real about what we are giving our attention to, because now we have to *feel* it. So how can we be sure if we are surrendering our attention to something that truly has our best interest at heart? Well, how does it make you feel? When you tell yourself that you do not and never will have enough time, love, money or opportunity, how does that make you feel? When you convince yourself that you need to foster a story, with your attention, that your butt is so big it is generating its own gravitational field, just to keep you from devouring another box of Twinkies, ask yourself how does that communication make you feel? Could there possibly be a kinder, gentler route one could navigate awareness through such as, "Body, beloved friend, I love you, I care for you, and I will only give you the highest food respect I can, because I value your health and well-being." How does the communication you give your attention to *feel?* The feeling feedback we get is the "keep it real" arena that Prime Source has blessed us with. If we monitor these feelings, we can minimize confusion and uncertainty.

When we run an inner dialogue that qualifies everyone on the freaking planet as having the I.Q. of an amoeba, except ourselves of course, how does that makes us feel? Frustrated? Annoyed? Superior in a mean spirited way? Giving our attention to a story that our personal Divinity is greater than the God consciousness of others clearly is not something running rampant among the Angels in Heaven. And what is it that makes us humans so vastly different from the Angels? The Angels are infinitely better practiced at policing their attention and arresting all non-Heavenly violators.

Swedenborg used to say that if we want to live in Heaven, we have to start practicing living there with our attention. If all we ever practice is seeing and living our lives as separate from the Angelic community, how will we ever find ourselves dwelling there? Swedenborg advises us to talk with the Angels, to give them our attention as an enlivened, love-devoted relationship, in our here and now reality. When we find ourselves entertaining anything outside of Heaven's Gate, simply hand it over to the Angels. Surrender to Heaven whatever does not belong in Heaven. Let go and let God recycle the energy into something more useful like happiness, a playful attitude and a generous Spirit.

What we give our attention to is the highest form of inner Spiritual alchemy available to anyone. The physical, outer-world based alchemy reality is simply a metaphor for turning the heaviest of our thoughts, the lead, into the purest gold of our focused attention. And unlike the arduous exterior atomic version of alchemy, the inner can be accomplished in an instant, in the blink of an eye, without expensive equipment, nasty bad smelling acids, or cluttered laboratories. Inner alchemy happens as quickly as it takes to release the dark and turn towards the Light. Another perk of inner alchemy is that all the inner gold you make, you actually get to take with you! I'd like to see Dupont Laboratories touch that one! (I may not be an alchemist or a scientist, but I did stay at a Holiday Inn last night.)

When you are watching your mind, your attention, you are also in the present moment. Being aware of where you are going with your mind, is like strapping on a seat belt that keeps you firmly in the here and now driver's seat. The times when you lose track of what you are doing with your attention is when you are most likely to start projecting off into the future, or withdrawing to relive some past event. Watching the flow of our awareness keeps the present moment on the radar screen. Letting the mind wander without consciousness to what you are loving, what you are making your God, is when the "you are here" red blip drops off the radar, and the plane starts to lose altitude. This is the entire purpose behind practicing any form of meditation; it keeps you in the now, watching the thoughts come up and practice letting them go. If you never practice opening your mind and letting go of your "stories", how will you have that skill when you need it?

Let's face it, most of us are extremely well versed in remaining as attached to our self-destructive, self-sabotaging thoughts as a great white shark is to its lunch. We bite down hard and fast and are determined to swallow everything, including the wrapper, whole. We need to become as proficient in the recognition of what is wasteful in our minds and attention and then releasing it, as we are in mindlessly accumulating the unwanted and the life diminishing. As they say in the business world, "you can't make chicken salad out of chicken sh*t". Watching what we are doing with our love supports us in detoxifying our minds and Spirit from our earlier unconscious, ignorant bad habits. It seems ironic that we give more attention to how our car affects our image, or what brand of beer we drink, than we do to how much of our attention we are freely returning to Heaven, so that we may live there!

Consider the expression "paying" attention. Like Swedenborg says, you love whatever you give your attention to. If you *pay* for it, you might as well get your *money's* worth. Are you paying for an "asset"? Are you getting a brand new Spiritual BMW? Or are your spiritual dollars going for a "liability", a broken down old Yugo that's got a rear window defroster for the sole purpose of keeping your hands warm while you push it to the repair shop, in knee deep snow during a winter freeze?

Aligning ourselves with the truth that you are what you love, and you love whatever you are giving your attention to, is why every Spiritual creature is having a physical experience. Having the Blessed opportunity to feel the truth of that higher Spiritual reality, in an arena we cannot fake, is why the Earth was created. Surrendering our free will and attention only and solely to what resides in Heaven, no matter what the physical world throws at you, is the life purpose of every person, everywhere, throughout all of time. If all of that is not enough to convince you that watching your attention is the definition of Spiritual maturity and success . . . then I've got some property in hell, uh, I mean on the outskirts of Heaven, I'd like to sell you!

Have You Got It?

*T*o quote the *Dhammapada*, (the sayings of the Buddha) "We are what we think. All that we are arises from our thoughts. With our thoughts we make the world." Or, as rephrased by *The Talking Heads*, "This ain't no party! This ain't no Disco! This ain't no fooling around!" Every person is a Spiritual creature that has come to the Earth to learn, to grow, in short ... to experience themselves as beyond limitation. The path to Spiritual maturity is not easy, and oftentimes it is not pretty. But it is necessary; it is the whole point of human existence. Every Spiritual tradition has offered words of wisdom to describe the sage, the evolved, the Spiritually mature. But in everyday life what does it look like? How does it respond to the pressures and stresses of everyday life? At the end of the day, what seduces our attention back into fear-based thoughts, and what infuses us with unconditional trust and acceptance in ourselves? Ultimately, what we give our attention to is what is essential. What we tell ourselves either justifies our undesirable behavior, or encourages us to trust in ourselves and require more of ourselves. Simply stated, we are what we love, and we love whatever we give our attention to. There is simply no way around that Spiritual Law ... that is why it is a Spiritual *LAW*, and not a Spiritual suggestion, or nice, warm and fuzzy, cute idea.

As the wisdom of *The Talking Heads* continues to remind us, "This ain't no Mud Club, or CBGB's, I ain't got time for that now!" Ultimately, we are all responsible for what we do with our consciousness — what actions we bring to bear as a result of our intentions. We are all here to get down to the Spiritual business of freeing our minds. To paraphrase the historical Buddha, "If you were in a burning building, you would not stop to ask, 'who started this fire? What type of accelerant did they use? What station or district will the fire trucks come from?' You would simply get down to the task of getting your charming butt out of the burning building!" So it is with Spiritual maturity. It does not matter what others are doing with their free will, how they are choosing to learn their lessons or get what they need to grow. All that matters is that you use your time here wisely, to free your mind from the burning building of life.

As the gospel according to David Byrne says, "I've lived in the Brownstone. I've lived in the ghetto. I've lived all over this town." We come here to experience the whole of life — to expand our understanding of ourselves through the medium of life in a 3-D world. In the Spiritual Realm there is no judgment, other than what we supply; there is simply choice. From what are we choosing to learn on a moment-to-moment basis? Are we choosing to learn from worry? Are we choosing to learn from intimidation and tantrum throwing? Are we choosing to learn from enthusiasm for life and love of play? When we choose, we determine where we live internally. When we choose to honor our expressions and the expressions of others, without judgment, we choose to live in a place free of fear. When we choose to grow as a result of trusting in ourselves as a force of Divine Love, when facing tough challenges, we live in an unlimited place. Or as the Dhammapada likes to say it, "It is better to conquer yourself than to win a thousand battles. Then the victory is yours. It cannot be taken from you, not by Angels or by demons, Heaven or hell."

"We dress like students. We dress like housewives, or in a suit and a tie. I've changed my hair style so many times now, I don't know what I look like." This is the rock and roll witness to the Buddhist Truth that this world is impermanent by nature. Everything here is in flux and change, because that is what life looks like on the third rock from the Sun. We come here to practice alignment with the eternal and unchanging reality of our True Nature, in a world completely void of what we really are. We come here to surrender our attention to what is unlimited and unchanging, while the limited world around us constantly gyrates and fluctuates. Achieving that requires us to focus our attention on the wisdom of the heart, while simultaneously liberating our minds from the tyranny of the ego. Spiritual maturity is mastering the habit of unconditionally perceiving, accepting and relating to ourselves and others as Divine Love, while being pummeled by every imaginable insidious condition life can assault us with. Or as the Dhammapada states, "The farmer channels water to his land. The fletcher whittles his arrows. And the carpenter turns his wood. So the wise man directs his mind."

Spiritual maturity is choosing to recognize only one power, while staring down the barrel of every fear you have ever fostered or nurtured. And this is the power of Divine Love and Wisdom. Spiritual maturity is trusting unflinchingly in the promised reality that no one, as Love, can create a learning experience they do not need, even while finding oneself going over Niagara Falls in a paper cup. Spiritual maturity is not for wussies or wimps. Spiritual maturity requires not taking the thoughts and actions of others personally. Spiritual maturity means letting others have the learning experience they came here to get, without standing on their karmic train tracks as the speeding engine of cause and effect comes barreling through. The Spiritually mature mind is tempered by the knowledge that it is not *what* we do that matters, but *why* we do it. In everyday life that translates into never labeling yourself as not good enough, when you know in your heart you showed up with pure and loving intentions. Spiritual maturity is a life that radiates from a core of Love, and is comforted by the truth that everything is as it should be. Life here on the Earth offers the Spiritually mature mind the opportunity to grow unconditionally, in an arena where we cannot fake it. The Spiritually mature mind above all values growth. It does not say to the wisdom suffering has brought us, "Stop making sense. Stop making sense, making sense, making sense."

Law of Attraction vs
Fatal Attraction

Unless you have been living under a rock, or isolated in a remote cave on a desert island, you have most likely found yourself in a conversation about the latest topic du jour: the Law of Attraction. The Law of Attraction looks like this:

Thoughts = Attraction

The truth of the matter is that the Law of Attraction is nothing new. It has been around as long as human consciousness. But thanks to the latest book and DVD, *The Secret,* this ancient idea is making a modern, popular resurgence. It does not matter whether or not you think all the hype is excrementally inclined, the buzz is in the air and it appears to be here for a while.

If you Google "the Law of Attraction" the information you get will describe it as the most powerful force in the universe. However, those who have traveled to the other side and come back to tell the tale, *all* say that Divine Love is the most powerful force in the universe. So who is right — Google or the Spiritual realm? Attention or Love? Well actually, they both are. We know this from the works of the great mystic Emanuel Swedenborg. What Swedenborg says is that we are what we love . . . and we love whatever we give our attention to. Our awareness, our attention, IS love. Emanuel Swedenborg further says that we do not have love; we ARE love, therefore whatever commands our attention ... we love. And, whatever we love, we ARE! We'll call this the Law of Love, and it looks like this:

$$You = Love = Attention = Love = You$$

Love is considered the most powerful universal force because it is wholeness making. In other words, it is the power of Love that will bring whatever you focus on into the *whole* of your life. This can be an extremely sobering reality, especially if you find yourself constantly drifting off into worry, lack, or fear-based thoughts. This means that you cannot spend 10 minutes a day focusing on copious quantities of money pouring into your bank account, and then work 23 hours and 50 minutes building a monument to scarcity with your attention, when you focus on thoughts like, "If only I had _____, (fill in the blank) everything would be okay," or, "why is it there are never enough hours in the day?" Your devoted love for "less" will out-weigh your casual flirtation with abundance. It would be like getting your nails done, and then spending the rest of the day biting them down to the quick. The cosmetic attention given to your nails would not stop the destructive end result of total ero-sion. Also, according to Swedenborg's wisdom, if this erosion or lack is where you focus your attention, this is also where you will be living: in a hellishly limited world. Not a pretty thought... which then manifests into your reality.

So, how can we use the Law of Love to improve our everyday life? First, we need to be aware of it. Secondly, if we are wise, we will be extremely judicious about what we are giving our at-tention to, because whatever it is, we will be attracting more of it into the whole of our life experience. And, thirdly, whenever we find ourselves focusing on *anything* limited, we need to immediately put it down, and return our attention to that which is unlimited. The bigger picture is that the Law of Attraction is really just a restatement of the Law of Love. The primary difference is that the Spiritual realm focuses on Love; the human, physical world focuses analytically on thoughts.

The Law of Attraction, because it is based on the Law of Love, will work to bring more life sustaining influences into the whole of your life, IF you do not spend the bulk of your life giving attention to some other fatal attraction. The Law of Love has an intimate relationship with our free will. Whatever we chose to freely love, we are also choosing to freely learn from. Emanuel Swedenborg says, in his prolific writings, that we are here having a human experience to learn that we gain nothing by giving our attention to anything limited. Furthermore, that we learn this truth as a result of what we have practiced freely giving our attention to over the course of our lives. The Law of Attraction works because we have the free will to decide, at any time, that we will give our attention only to what lives in an unlimited place.

Whenever we find ourselves entertaining something limiting with our mind, only we have the free will to put down that thought and return our attention to what is beyond limitation. As Emanuel Swedenborg liked to say, giving attention exclusively to the unlimited is a remembering and a forgetting thing. You have to remember to give your attention to what is unlimited, and simply forget everything else.

It is not "The Secret"...
It is "The Best Kept Secret"

*T*he idea that whatever we give our attention to has power is nothing new, contrary to what's implied by the title to the latest book and DVD, "The Secret". Over two hundred and fifty years ago, Emanuel Swedenborg phrased "The Secret" as:

> You are what you love; and you love whatever you give your attention to. You do not have Divine Consciousness; you *are* Divine Consciousness. And how you direct that Consciousness opens the door to either Heaven or hell.

For some obscure reason, however, the wisdom of this amazing man is a greater secret than "The Secret's" secret.

The fact that very few people seem to be aware of the over 35 volumes of his work, the over one million words that have been in constant publication since they were originally written, would make the wisdom of Emanuel Swedenborg not just a secret, but the ultimate in best kept secrets!

So what does the best kept secret want us to know? Well, for starters we are all here for one reason ... and it has nothing to do with manifesting a red Lamborghini in your driveway. It has nothing to do with being obsessed with how big your butt is. It has nothing to do with whatever the Home Shopping Network is telling you to buy in order to be fulfilled. Stumped? The secret behind the secret is that we are all here to learn more about Divine Love and Wisdom! Not what you thought, I bet.

Learning more about Divine Love and Wisdom is the big picture truth. Don't get caught up or be distracted by the little things that you feel do not go your way. The bigger picture, the bigger "Law of Attraction" is that you do not have Divine Love and Wisdom; you *are* Divine love and Wisdom. The planet Earth is the place Spiritual creatures having a human experience come to practice BEING one with their Spiritual Identity, which is Divine love and Wisdom, no matter what life delivers to your driveway. Don't bother looking now; the red foreign car still isn't there. (And by the way, you can't attract something you can't spell either, so maybe you need to shoot for a red Kia.)

In our human experience, the body comes complete with a nervous system. (Well, not really complete – batteries not included, and there is no instruction manual or warranty.) The nervous system makes this physical existence an arena that we cannot fake it in. Here you have to "feel" the gyrations of life. Life is constantly inviting us to realize ourselves, unconditionally:

Can you be love now?

It's easy when you get the red Lamborghini in you garage, but . . .

Can you be love now?

Even when the closest you get is being run over by a red sports car?

No matter what life throws at you . . .

Can you be love now?

Forget the red sports car or at the very least do not let it domi-
nate or eclipse your purpose for being here altogether! You are
here to learn more about Divine Love and Wisdom, and the
biggest thing you are here to learn about it is: that you do not
have Divine Love and Wisdom; you *are* Divine Love and Wisdom . . . no matter what unexpected surprises you encounter.
You *are* Divine Love and Wisdom *unconditionally*. Trust me,
life will offer you every opportunity to practice this under every possible circumstance. Your job is to attract the unflinching,
heartfelt response that you *can* be Love now!

When I teach classes on the Law of Attraction a'la Swedenborg,
I start out asking, "If you are interpreting struggle, life-altering
challenges and the experience of unpleasant or painful situations
as meaning that you are Spiritually inept, stupid or doing the
'Law of Attraction' wrong, we need to talk." Riddle me this: if
a life fraught with pain and suffering means you are a Spiritual
"Law of Attraction" dropout, then Jesus must have been the biggest loser of them all! If you have not been betrayed by those
closest to you, as well as by your countrymen, if you have not
been arrested, convicted of treason, tortured and crucified, then
you fall somewhere under the suffering bar that Jesus has raised
for us all. And yet, if you know in your heart that this is *not* true,
Jesus is *not* the biggest Spiritual screw-up on the planet, then
something is deeply wrong with this paradigm. The misleading
factor is understanding the illusion of life for what it is, and
choosing instead to embrace the truth that sets us free!

The question is not, "Why are bad or challenging things happening to me?" Is not the planet Earth where we come to grow, to practice getting over our loyalty to limitation, and to practice unconditional love in an arena that we cannot fake? After all, **the greater the student, the greater the lesson.** Nelson Mandela, Martin Luther King Jr., Gandhi, Mother Teresa, Homer Simpson, Joan of Arc - none of them had a charmed life. **The question is not why are bad things happening, the question is how does one respond to these challenging things!** Do we choose to respond with, **"Yes, I can still be Love now!"** or do we choose something infinitely more limiting, not to mention less Spiritually fashionable? As Swedenborg tells us in his Divinely guided wisdom, only what we need to reach enlightenment is allowed to touch us. There are profound seeds of transformational growth within all suffering. We all experience pain in life. Oftentimes, however, the *level* of suffering is optional. As God Consciousness, no one can create a learning experience they do not need! You can trust that you are Divine Love and Divinely Loved, unconditionally! So, put that in your red Lamborghini and hit the road.

What is Spirituality About Anyway?

*S*pirituality today gets such a bad rap. I've actually heard people refer to it as the "s" word. It conjures up images of people who appear to be on some type of Valium, speaking in breathy voices, wearing long flowing robes, waving smoking wands of incense or sage in one hand, and brandishing a large crystal in the other. If you asked the proverbial "man on the street" about his perception of Spirituality, here's what you'd most likely hear:

- Someone expounding about Eastern concepts like "chakras," "auras," "rising kundalini" and "mantras".

- A small group of people who insist they are going to Heaven, and no one else is.

- People who read astrological charts to determine who or what is in Uranus, or why my Mercury is in retrograde or your Escalade is in for a brake job.

- Guys with orange robes and shaved heads banging on tambourines while holding out collection plates at your local airport.

- Sister Geneva who sits in a candle lit room filled with incense smoke dealing out cards and turning some face up, while looking at you and shaking her head. (Personally, I've never seen Texas Hold'em played like that before, and I never can tell when she's bluffing.)

- The people in the supermarket newspapers who claim they are having an alien's baby while being mind-controlled by our Government through the chip in their cell phone.

- Lastly, the Psychic Hotline.

The truth of the matter is spirituality has nothing to do with what kind of clothes a person wears, or how many hours one sits cross-legged in the lotus position, perched upon a mediation pillow. Spirituality is not dependent upon whether or not you read tarot cards while sporting stylish crystal jewelry, or whether or not you accept the notion of life on other planets. Spirituality is not a fad, a style of fashion, a club that you join, a practice involving rocks, feathers or the amassing of any other ceremonial accessories. Spirituality is not achieved by attending a drumming circle, claiming a "born again" status, or having anointed yourself with holy ash from India. Spirituality has nothing to do with any kind of "doing" or belief system at all.

Emanuel Swedenborg explained it the best, when he wrote that spirituality is *life* itself. Without spirit there is no life. When spirit enters any physical form, this is what we call the beginning of life. When spirit departs from its temporal housing, this is what we call death. But that is only death of the *physical* body. Swedenborg goes on to explain that "life" exists before the procurement of your present carbon based bag of protoplasm, and it exists long after that packaging has fallen away (after that "library book" has been returned). That "life," that "spirit" is timeless and immortal, constantly growing and evolving. One might even go so far as to say that the only two consistent and constant things are life and growth.

This means we are all guilty of spirituality; we have all committed the "s" word. Every moment, for all eternity, we are one with spirituality, no matter how tasteless or offensive that may seem to you now. But take heart, for Swedenborg says that we all come direct from the manufacturer with free will. That is our Divine birthright! (And that is way better than the 12-month parts and labor extended warranty option.) That means that you get to choose what kind of life you will lead. Will it be one that recognizes only one power: divine love and wisdom? One that is centered on the honest caring and valuing of all life . . . all spirituality? Will it be a life that is devoted to being happy, staying happy, and propagating happiness? Or will it be a life focused incessantly on the flaws, limitations, criticisms and sources of unhappiness? You get to decide with . . . yes . . . that's right . . . your spirituality. You vote with your life.

So what is spirituality about anyhow? It is about life, pure and simple. But what Oscar Wilde said of truth can be said about life: it is never pure and rarely simple. Fortunately, Oscar Wilde being the dispenser of rare insightful gems that he is, offered us more direct advice on life and learning, when he said, "Life is never fair . . . and perhaps it is good thing for most of us that it is not." And "Nothing is good in moderation. You cannot know good in anything till you have torn the heart out of it by excess." And then there is my ultimate favorite, "Life is much too important a thing to ever talk seriously about."

What have we established in our search for the truth about spirituality? Well, we now know for sure that "rising kundalini" is not a vegetarian dish in an Indian restaurant; crystals, tarot cards, and singing meditation bowls are all fun, but they do not make anyone more spiritual than anyone else. We have all committed the "s" word, and will continue to do so until time immemorial. And if you do not know what life or reality is . . . please . . . do not take it seriously! Hello, Psychic Hotline???

Many Names, One God

*T*oday more than ever the effects of religious conflict can be felt in global episodes of tension and violence. Suicide bombers expect a Heavenly sponsored orgy as a reward for murdering innocent people; family members alienate family members, because their religious beliefs and expressions differ from one another, or from a traditional norm. The tragedy that clinging to a rigid "buy or die" or "my way or the highway" belief system creates, is that it disenfranchises us, individually and collectively, from the truth. And exactly what truth is that, you may ask? Emmanuel Swedenborg said it better than any one else, when he reminded us that there is only one God. It does not matter what name you call that God, or what point in time you worshipped that God, there is only the one God. That means we are **all** worshipping the same God, no matter how different our expression or ritualized behavior appears to be.

In the fashion world, accessories make the outfit. The religious world is not any different. Most religious organizations share an equal passion for clinging to the accessories that make their denominational "outfit" stand out and apart from others. If you find yourself in the Catholic fashion club, then you will find that getting baptized is a religious must for your group. If you are a practicing Hindu, you are more than likely also a vegetarian. Buddhists shave their heads after making a serious commitment to their awakened Buddha Nature. Accessorize the bald head with an orange robe and tambourine, and you have haute couture of the 60's airports. If you are a Muslim, you face Mecca to pray numerous times a day, and as a Muslim woman, you most likely also have your head covered. There's also a good chance your daughter will not be participating in the "wet burka" contest at the downtown Islamabad Hooters. Oh, and if you are entered as one of God's "chosen people", that doesn't guarantee a win either.

For me, personally, humor is my Holy sacrament of choice. I refer to myself as Pope Hilarious II, from the Church of the Hilarious, where stand up comics are prophets, and the three stooges are my three wise guys — I mean men. Right Moe?

Bearing in mind Swedenborg's wisdom that there is only one God, means that in the larger scheme of things, we have much more in common than in diversity, no matter what secret password, handshake or fashion wear your club promotes. We are all seeking communion with the same Source. We are all sharing the same Spiritual zip code. We are all reaching out through the vehicle of our lives and love to touch the face of the one God. How cool is that!

Is it just me, or doesn't focusing on our collective unity make the greatest, wisest, most life enhancing sense? Once we realize we are all playing with the same Barbie doll, she is just dressed differently, so to speak, then it would follow that tolerance, understanding and exploring a healthy curiosity will emerge naturally, without effort or pretense. Granted we would have to give up cute little sayings like "We must kill the infidels, but first let's stop at McDonalds" or "God will forgive you if you say 10 Hail Marys". And of course the ever popular, "If you love Jesus, send $10 to the address shown on the bottom of your TV screen" would become passé overnight. But I suspect we could all live quite comfortably with these minor changes. And, needless to say, it would probably make for a substantially more relaxed social exchange once we surrendered any and all self-created airs, posturing and inferences of superiority. Yes, indeed, all we have to lose would be our myopic perspectives and narrow-minded values. All in all not a bad exchange for finally being able to recognize our Spiritual brothers and sisters.

Just think about how emotionally satisfying it will be to see Oral Roberts embracing the Dali Lama as an equal in Heaven's community. Or the warm fuzzy feeling that would come over you while watching a Sikh asking a Taoist to show him how to connect to perfect nothingness. It would bring a smile to your face to see an Islamic extremist trading in his AK-47 for an apple strudel at a Jewish bakery and getting it at wholesale! Visualize an American Indian Shaman walking into an Eastern Indian Hindu home, seeing all the statues of Shiva and Krishna everywhere and responding with, "I am so touched by the profound devotion you have for Great Spirit." Atheists everywhere would be throwing in the towel as well, because there would be such a global party happening, they would not want to be left out. At the very least they would be hedging their bet. And last but not least, there would be the ubiquitous recognition of the tax-free status of Pope Hilarious II. People everywhere would be Blessing each other with seltzer water and jokes. Yes! Imagine a world where no one has to prove or fight over whose God is greater, more powerful or better looking. The copasetic cooperative possibilities are absolutely as endless as . . . as . . . the worship of God itself!

Long live Pope Hilarious II.

Never Be in the Present
Moment without "IT"

*T*here is an aspect of each one of us that never changes, never ages, never dies. There is a feature in every human being that is infinite, unlimited and permanent in nature. Obviously, IT is not our good looks, charming personality or athletic ability. Clearly we do not see IT, and we don't see IT clearly either. We neither smell IT, taste IT, nor hear IT. We also can't seem to touch IT. So what is IT? Where is this immortal, impermeable portion of the program? How do we get to IT? Where is IT hiding? The answer is . . . where most of us are least likely to look for *IT* . . . *inside.* IT is awareness itself.

Awareness is that force of attention, that energy which is constantly watching, witnessing the movement of life as it parades in front of us. Awareness is the doorway to perception. Awareness is that part of us that feels the same when we are five, and when we are ninety-five. Awareness is the only dimension of ourselves that we take with us, regardless of the functional condition of the body — dead or alive, comatose or intensely focused. Awareness is the mojo that determines who is enlightened and who is a dim bulb. Awareness is the only thing about us that is real and authentic. IT is the testimony and proof of God's existence. After all, where does awareness come from? Can awareness come from an absence of awareness?

One of the many ironies about awareness is that we do not have

IT; we cannot lose it, or report it as stolen, because we *are IT*! We *are* awareness itself, and yet we can be so unaware of our awareness, all at the same time. What happens when we drive and talk on the cell phone? Awareness of the present moment road conditions evaporates in an instant. We ¨wake up¨ miles later, incognizant of what transpired in the missing miles. Unfortunately, some people go through life like this — on autopilot. Awareness, like life itself, requires that we own it and operate it properly. It would seem that photocopy machines are not the only things that suffer from "operator failure."

When you do not control your mind, it controls you. This is often times a source of great embarrassment and suffering. For example, the open fly, or dragging around the odd piece of toilet paper stuck to the bottom of your shoe. There is a practice, in Buddhism, where the teacher sneaks around a group of students and suddenly whacks one on the back of the legs with a stick. If your mind was wandering, not being aware, this will bring you back to the present moment faster than you can say, "Shiva H. Vishnu! What the f··k are you doing?" (I know, I know, that's a Hindu expression, but when have you ever heard a Buddhist swear?) The idea behind this little spiritual S & M ritual is that IF your awareness was present, you would not have gotten whacked in the first place. The sting of the stick is the teacher's way of asking the student, "This is the present moment, do you know where your awareness is?"

There are more profound and skill-developed tricks of the consciousness trade such as lucid dreaming, astral projection, and remote viewing. These all require focusing awareness, concentrating IT on whatever the task is that you are performing - being here now, without disenfranchising the flow of awareness along the way. Even the Army understands this, with slogans like "Be all that you can be" and "An army of one." Well, you cannot "be" all that you can "be", and "be" unaware of what you are doing with your attention at the same time. An army of one is a unified mind; the military just has a slightly different focus on that purpose and intention than our Buddhist buddy with the stick. Let's face it; if the army gets IT, IT should be a no-brainer for the rest of us. No offense to the army, it's just not famous for attracting spiritual seekers who are looking to liberate their minds through a nonviolent version of the "know thyself" quest.

Distraction seems to be a very popular drug of choice these days. And it is very easy to get a daily "fix" from your computer, MP3 player, cell phone, video game, or Blackberry. Our thoughts always seem to be supported in wandering elsewhere. The Spirit is willing, but the attention is weak. Going through life unaware is how we have all contributed to some of the greatest problems on the Earth today. Being here now, showing up for the present moment aware and awake, might just be the global panacea we are all craving. Now, if we can just remember to remember where our awareness is, we should be just fine. The good news is . . . that maybe we left IT with our car keys. Happy motoring!

Section 4 ~ Mind/Body/Spirit

Meditation: It's Not What You Think

*I*t was the great Spiritual teacher J. Krishnamurti, who once said, "If you think that meditation is sitting in a corner of your room for fifteen to twenty minutes, and then getting up and paying no attention to the rest of your day, you are *not* meditating. You are *fooling yourself!*" What does he mean by this? Meditation is the process of watching the mind, paying attention to where it wanders, and then bringing it back to a place or point of focus. The point of focus can be watching the breath; it can be holding a mantra or a specifically designed intention or thought. When we devote a small amount of time in our day to paying attention to where the mind wanders, and then spend the rest of our waking moments letting the mind run chaotically around, we are not "getting" what meditation is all about. We are, as Krishnamurti so dramatically pointed out, merely fooling ourselves.

It was the great scientist/mystic Emanuel Swedenborg who first originated the phrase, *"You are what you love, and you love whatever you give your attention to."* What this means is that our awareness is a form of love. Love is not limited to what we like or feel we have an affinity for. Love is inseparable from our awareness. When we give something our attention, we are also giving it our love. Love, being the most profound force in the Universe, will bring more of whatever it is we are giving our attention to, into the whole of our life. The purpose of meditation is to awaken to what we are giving our love to - to become conscious of what we love, by virtue of giving it our attention.

How this Spiritual Law, *"You are what you love, and you love whatever you give your attention to"* translates into our everyday life is this: when you give your attention to worry, self-criticism, or bad faith in life and love, then you actually love being stressed out, "less than" and a victim. Shocking isn't it! We perceive these things as something we do not love, something we would like to avoid, and something we do not want in our lives. However, if you are giving them your attention, you *are* inviting more of the same into your life.

Meditation is a practice designed to support us in the process of catching our mind when it wanders off, and seeing where it goes. By doing this, while we are caught up in the flow and unconscious habituation of everyday life, we gradually become more and more aware of what we are doing with our love. Meditation is supposed to be a way in life; it is not supposed to be an action that lives in a vacuum. Meditation is a template, used to hone the skill of making your mind your best friend and not your worst enemy.

Meditation activates an inner alarm system that draws our attention back to the bigger questions of life: *"Is what I am presently giving my attention to what I really what I want to be doing with my love? Is what I am thinking about really the best use of my love, right here, right now? Did I come here to the Earth to build a monument to worry and unhappiness with my love? Or do I choose to empower something else with my love, something infinitely more life sustaining."* All of us have been Blessed with the gift of Free Will. Each of us decides what we choose to do with our attention, and what attitude we choose as a response to life.

In the midst of working, driving, shopping, refueling at the coffee spot . . . while in the throws of everyday life, this is when we need to be aware of where the mind is wandering off. Can we make it through the day consciously catching our attention as it plunges off into negativity and limitation and bring it back? Or will we sleepwalk through our lives, letting our attention bounce around like a winning shot on a pinball machine? Without understanding the importance of judiciously watching what we give our attention to, we will never get the balance and power out of meditation that it is designed to bring into our lives. Without connecting the Spiritual Law, *"You are what you love, and you love whatever you give your attention to"* to the intention and action of meditation, you will be reducing meditation to a tacky, new age cliché.

Ultimately, meditation is about holding the awareness that we can *be* love in every moment of our lives. Meditation is here to support us in not getting distracted by the things happening within or without us. It is here to hold fast to aligning our attention to the truth that we are Divine Love and Wisdom in this and every moment, and that no one and no thing has the power to change that. When you can hold that "love of the truth" with your attention, meditation has served its purpose - to help you embody being the unconditional Love you are, no matter what the world throws at you. Meditation is the soft quiet voice that reminds you, *"You are what you love, and you love whatever you give your attention to . . . so Love wisely."*

How Spiritually Healthy Are You?

*T*oday we have many sophisticated diagnostic tools available to help us determine our bone density, the iron content of our blood, and even the functional capacity of our internal organs. We even have tests to measure our depression, our tendency toward bipolar disorder, or ADD. However, our level of Spiritual health is rarely, if ever, examined. Since we are all Spiritual creatures having an "embodied" experience, it would make tremendous sense not to overlook what is the permanent and eternal aspect of our true nature. After all, our emotional and physiological health really falls under the umbrella of our Spiritual health. So how does one go about a Spiritual self-examination to determine the vitality of our God Consciousness?

There are actually three tests we can perform to discern the level of our Spiritual health, or the health of anyone else for that matter. Surprised? Don't be. We all came to the Earth to engage in what Socrates called the great "know thyself" quest, and to know thyself consciously, as a Spiritual being, is the best that quest gets!

The first thing we want to examine is our perception. This is going to be a bit more challenging than the "turn your head and cough" exam you had in high school gym class. The results depend on how honest we are willing to be about our internal dialogue: what we tell ourselves about our relationship with Divine love, and our value, power and worth. As Emanuel Swedenborg used to say, "You do not have love . . . you are love." Love is not a possession. Love is not separate from who and what you are. Love is not earned; it is embodied. There are no issue hurdles that determine if we are finally deserving and worthy enough to be loved. We do not have love, we are love. Deserving and worthy have never been an issue, unless we make it an issue with what we do with our perception.

Although we have a body, we *are* awareness. We do not have awareness; we are it. Furthermore, our awareness *is* our Divinity. It is the part of us that is eternal and unchanging. Our awareness is the part of us that feels it never ages. Therefore, whatever we give our attention to is what we infuse with our God energy. How healthy you are Spiritually depends completely on:

How much attention you give to the Truth about your Divinity

How much separation you make from the tyranny of your own ego, and the lies it fabricates out of ignorance and the need for self-preservation.

Emanuel Swedenborg used to say that being Spiritually healthy was a matter of remembering and forgetting. Remembering to give your attention to the Truth and forgetting everything else. Forgetting all the Puritan work ethic programming, forgetting your own self-perpetuating stories of unlovable and inept. Forgetting everything that does not align itself with the Truth that you do not have love . . . *you are love!* For the sake of this mutual sharing we are going to define Heaven as a place or state of being that is unlimited, and hell as a place or state of being that is limited. Swedenborg suggests that we give our attention solely to what resides in Heaven. Should we find ourselves entertaining something limited with our attention, Swedenborg suggests we put it down, forget it, and give our attention back to Heaven. When we surrender our awareness to what lives in Heaven, our Spiritual health is unlimited. When we give our attention to what lives in hell, our Spiritual health will immediately become extremely, extremely limited.

How much of the time do you practice owning your Divinity and giving your attention to Heavenly things such as good faith in life and love, and respecting yourself as a force of love? Do you see yourself as reaching enlightenment the fastest most efficient way you can, to the exclusion of all other stories? If you do, this will also tell you the Spiritual health of your free will. Each of us decides where we go with our attention. Divine Love and Wisdom saw fit to give each person sovereignty over his/her own mind. So how much of your attention you freely surrender back to Prime Source, will tell you the health of your free will, or what Swedenborg called your 'Ruling Love'.

The second litmus test for Spiritual health is the relationship test. How healthy are your relationships? Remember honesty counts! Every person on the planet *is* God consciousness. We do not have it; we *are* it. Since all of us are an expression of God consciousness, how we treat other people is how we treat God. You can take all the vitamins you want, eat healthy, fresh foods, exercise regularly, drink plenty of water, sleep eight hours nightly, but if you go through your day criticizing yourself and others, finding fault and blame in yourself and others, intimidating, disrespecting or bullying others, gossiping from a mean spirited heart, or withholding help and compassion from others, then you are deeply Spiritually unhealthy. Disenfranchising God consciousness is a Spiritual illness, and the primary symptom of this malady is unhappiness.

Conversely, someone like Christopher Reeves can be in a wheelchair, neurologically damaged beyond repair, yet still be incredibly Spiritually healthy, because of the quality of his love and generosity of Spirit. The great love teacher, Jesus, encouraged everyone to be Spiritually healthy when he asked us to love our enemies and treat others as we would want to be treated. Dannion Brinkley, in his powerful, best selling autobiography, *Saved By The Light*, talks about being struck by lightening and being clinically dead for over thirty minutes. Dannion frankly discusses his experiences on the other side and the panoramic life review that awaits us all. He describes having to *feel* the impact he had on *all* his relationships as the primary educator of his and everyone's Soul. Because we are all connected by Prime Source, what we do to another, we have done to God. There is simply no getting around this as a determinate of how Spiritually healthy we are.

This brings us to our last test; our last self-examinational procedure. God Consciousness is very, very creative. God created the Heavens and the Earth. God creates something from nothing. We are here on Earth to create enlightenment from ignorance. Healthy God consciousness is creative. When we are Spiritually healthy we are creating a new response to old issues, and growing beyond them. Unhealthy God consciousness recreates the old issues: the limited suffering over and over again, without breaking the cycle, without expanding beyond the grasp of unhappiness.

Take a step back and objectively look at your life. How often are you recreating your old issues? You know the old, outdated sources of suffering you love so much to indulge in: worrying, telling yourself you'll never be happy or truly loved, building a monument with your awareness to how there is never going to be enough time, love, money or opportunity. Ask yourself how often are you recreating these stories, these perceptions? How often do you reach for the worry drug of choice and justify the addiction? How often do you defend your existence as rejected, alone and miserable? Giving your attention to these issues consistently produces results that guarantee your unhappiness, yet you still find yourself drinking from this cup. This dysfunction is unhealthy God consciousness habitually recreating its limiting issues, beyond the point of reason or usefulness.

No one can lament an abandoned life of rejected loneliness and, at the same time, know that they do not have love; they *are* love. No one can be experiencing themselves as incompetent, incapable and a loser, and, at the same time, know that they do not have value, power and worth; they *are* value, power and worth.

No one can be recreating a limited story and be creating a new response to it at the same time. It would be a contradiction. No one took a body and came to the Earth to build a monument to crap and self-delusion. We all came here to realize that we *are* Divine love and absolutely nothing else!

If you practice being creative, you are strengthening your Spiritual health. All of us have mastery over anything only after practice. If you practice being creative, simply for the sake of being creative, you are practicing aligning yourself with the intelligence you need to create enlightenment. If you practice being creative for the sake of being creative, you will have the skill when you need it, because you have practiced cultivating it. Without some relationship of practicing responding to life creatively, how will anyone be able to create a new response to old, ingrained responses?

Recreating our issues over and over again ad nauseum is to align ourselves with fear, and there is unquestionably nothing Spiritually healthy about that.

Like any other form of health, we come to the Earth to practice right relationship with it. Spiritual health can always been improved with loving attention. The good news is there are no insurance premiums, no gym fees to pay, no restrictive diets, and no personality tests to fail. Spiritual health is every being's birthright. All we have to do is claim it, live it, share it, and shine on!

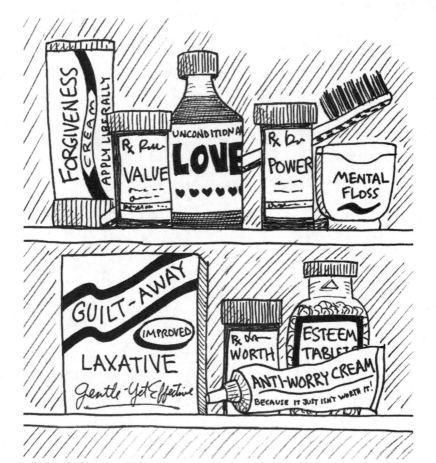

Spiritual Healing . . .
It's All in Your Head

When faced with a need to resolve a physical condition, no one ever says, "I am dealing with a carbon based dilemma. I need a biologically oriented panacea." So, what separates a spiritual healing from a corporeal relevant reality? Only our perception of the event. The truth of the matter is that we all existed as Spiritual creatures long before our bags of protoplasm appeared on the planet, and we will exist long after our Earthly packaging has fallen to the wayside. Our consciousness, our awareness is our Spiritual Nature, and it is designed to drive the physical, not the other way around. Our body is constructed to organize its intelligence around how our Spiritual Nature directs it.

Spiritual healing starts with perception - what we are giving our attention to. Coincidentally, this is where Spiritual dis-ease begins as well. It was Emanuel Swedenborg who stated it with precision when he wrote that a plethora of fears, insecurities, worries, neuroses and psychoses could be healed by knowing who and what we are. Of course, the implication is that we acquire the need for healing as a result of not knowing who and what we are. My mother always told me I should get my head examined. Looks like she was right.

Over two hundred years ago Swedenborg first conceived the phrase *you are what you love and you love whatever you give*

your attention to. The idea is that our awareness, our consciousness, and our Divinity are inseparable from love. That means
that whatever we give our attention to, we are also imbuing with
the most powerful force in the Universe — love! In practice,
aligning ourselves with the truth about whom and what we are
happens via our perception of ourselves. So when we give our
attention to, "I'm the person who always loses the lottery, I'm
always in the slowest lane on the freeway, or no matter what I
wear, it always makes my butt look bigger than the Goodyear
blimp," then we love being less than, inferior and unlovable . . .
shocking isn't it?

It is no wonder that limited, dysfunctional self-identification
ultimately results in mental and emotional illness. "Garbage in
. . . garbage out", as my trash man, who also works in high tech,
articulates it. In actuality, these thought provoking illnesses are
designed to act as a wake-up call. To awaken us to the reality
that in no uncertain terms, we have surrendered our attention to
fallacies, erroneous beliefs about our true nature, and to invite us
to exchange these stories for the truth.

So what exactly is the truth about our Spiritual/human identity?
Swedenborg said it better than anyone else when he said that
we do not *have* love. Love is not a possession. It cannot be lost
or stolen, bent, folded, stapled or mutilated. You cannot find it
on eBay. I checked. The auction expired two hours ago. Only
kidding. Love is not a commodity to be traded for or bargained
with. We do not have love . . . we *are* love. Love is our very
being. And when we know this no matter how many bad dates
and ugly divorces, or ugly dates and bad divorces we go through,
we never let our divinity suffer as a result. We never regress into
"not good enough" or "unlovable."

As pure love, that means that we do not have value, power and worth; we *are* value, power and worth. When did love ever lack for value, power, worth...or anything for that matter? We no longer need to wait until family members or coworkers throw a few small "you finally have some value" crumbs our way. We are not dependent upon our financial or social status for power. It is ours for the claiming.

How many times has a situation like not being able to pay your bills, getting fired from a job, or just not getting that promotion robbed you of your self- esteem and sense of worth? When you do not know who and what you are, you are vulnerable to the gyrations of the temporal world. When you are aligned with the eternal truth of your Spiritual/human identity, you weather the storms of outrageous misfortune with your oneness to Divine love completely and unconditionally intact.

Swedenborg further develops this wisdom by asking us to expand this trust in ourselves and our lives, based on this identification with love. To get to the next level, Swedenborg points out that we do not have God Consciousness; we *are* God Consciousness, because when was love ever separate from God? Then he asks, "How can God create a learning experience of itself it did not need?" God is capable of many things, but creating a useless, un-necessary learning experience is not one of them. Furthermore, we cannot create that experience before or after we needed it. You get what you need, when you need it. That means that we can show up fearlessly for our lives, knowing that essentially, everything we experience is working for us! It is all designed for the evolution of our Souls, for the benefit of our greater growth, or it would not be allowed to touch our lives! Swedenborg says Divine Love and Wisdom promises us that we are, in fact, reaching enlightenment the fastest, most efficient way we can. As love, we do not have the ability to do anything else.

Imagine a life where you are senior to every life challenge. These difficulties have come to serve you. Visualize yourself as pure Divine love and absolutely nothing else. Internalize a story that you do not have value, power and worth; you *are* it. And no one or no thing on this planet has the power to change that. Now aren't you feeling better already?

What's Enlightenment Got to Do with It?

*E*very year seems to bring greater technological advancements, more expansive CNN coverage of the latest fear du jour, and trendier fashions that will be forgotten in less than six months time. We seem to give less and less consideration to what is ultimately enduring and timeless, such as human consciousness. So why is it that the most complex wonder of all, enlightenment, the miracle of awareness itself, is rarely considered a priority in refinement?

Is it because enlightenment is not modeled for us individually and collectively as much as Jessica Simpson's double D's are? Perhaps it is because enlightenment has gotten a bad rap as being dull in comparison to the last gameboy, playstation or MP3 player. Or maybe it is because possessing more toys has become more valuable than acquiring life transcending wisdom. Whatever the reason, it's about time we downloaded the latest "enlightenment" upgrade file onto the hard drive of our daily lives. After all, this is about the most important relationship we will ever know: no, not the relationship with our 401K; no, not the relationship with the waitresses down at Hooters; but rather the much neglected relationship we have with our own minds.

Is your mind your best friend or your worst enemy? Imagine what life would be like if we never questioned that we are in fact completely deserving and worthy of love right now . . . just as we are. What if we never mistrusted our capabilities - our value, power and worth? Not ever. No, not even if we got dumped by the best lay we ever knew! Not even if we gained a few pounds, discovered more hair in the bathroom sink than on our heads, gained a few more pounds, or, on further review, saw that the hair in the bottom of the sink was gray. What if we knew unconditionally we could never be separate from love? For one, Rodney Dangerfield would have never said, "I could tell my parents hated me. My bath toys were a toaster and a radio."

What would our daily lives feel like if we knew, beyond a shadow of a doubt, that we do not have love we *are* love? How would our lives change if we no longer believed we had to wait until our family, coworkers or friends finally told us we were now deserving and worthy of love? How many neurotic habits could we just let go of if we never had to prove we were good enough for anything ever again?

Enlightenment, after all, is really about love and our relationship with it. Think of all the time and resources we could save if we realized that our relationship with love and worth was never in jeopardy; no matter what changes our physical packaging went through, or how well we performed the 'stupid human tricks' of our everyday lives?

What if we were so intoxicated with our own self-respect that we no longer needed to compare ourselves to anyone else? What if each and every present moment was experienced as having our best interest at heart?

Emanuel Swedenborg used to say that enlightenment is not a doing thing, it is a remembering and a forgetting thing. In other words, we do not reach enlightenment by doing something. If doing were the doorway to enlightenment, then every workaholic would be fully self-realized by now, and clearly that is not the case. No, it is not an accomplishment achieved through doing.

What Swedenborg is saying is that the purpose of human existence is for us to realize that there is nothing useful in giving our attention to anything limiting. He says that we are here to practice giving our attention to what dwells in an unlimited place, to the exclusion of all other thoughts. He says that the best way to live that, is to remember the truth:

> You do not have Divine love; you *are* Divine love.
> You do not have value, power and worth; you *are*
> value, power and worth.
> And simply forget everything else.

Swedenborg goes on to say that because we do not have God Consciousness, we *are* God Consciousness, we cannot create a learning experience we do not need. He asks, "How can God Consciousness create a learning experience of itself, it did not need?" God Consciousness apparently has the power to do a lot of things, but create something it did not need is not one of them. Swedenborg encourages all of us to remember that we are all working towards enlightenment the fastest most efficient way that we can. We do not have the power to do anything else. This means putting down all our old tired stories about how we, or others, did not do it right, or are not good enough; setting aside our deeply ingrained habit of criticizing others and ourselves. Imagine what life would be like if everyone remembered to trust in themselves and in the self-corrective power of their Divinity?

Wouldn't it be interesting if you could experience the Holidays and upcoming New Year with a mind that remembers to accept itself and others for the Divine force of love we all truly are. It might mean the conversations around the dinner table and family gatherings will have to change. There would no longer be the "idiot" cousin or brother. The retelling of how some family member is a "loser" would have to end. I suspect a few of the "in-law" jokes and "lawyer" jokes might take a while to die a natural death. But wouldn't it be interesting to see what effect remembering the truth would have on our minds, our relationships and our experience of the present moment.

Free will dictates that we all get to choose for ourselves what we do with our attention. We decide whether we will build a monument to limitation and fear, or if we choose to align our attention with the higher reality that we are now, and always have been, one with Divine love. As Swedenborg likes to say there are Spiritual laws, just as there are physical world laws, and one of those Spiritual laws is: you are what you love, and you love whatever you are giving your attention to. Remember only you can make the choice to love wisely.

The Universal Language

No matter what your background, style of self-expression or fashion preference — pentagram, crystals, bra-less, or broom, there is a Universal language that transcends dogma, ideologies, belief systems and rituals. It existed before the Pagans, Wiccans, Christianity, Druids, or Moonies. It is the language of love. But what actually is love? In its essence, it is consciousness, our awareness. "You are what you love, and you love whatever you give your attention to" is how Emanuel Swedenborg phrased it over two hundred years ago. He coined the definitive phrase because he understood that we do not have love; we *are* love! And as we career headlong into the twenty-first century, no one yet has managed to say it better.

Many people have heard of Dannion Brinkley, Sylvia Brown, Edgar Cayce and Nostradamus. Yet most people today have never heard of Emanuel Swedenborg, unless they went to seminary or received an advanced degree in religious philosophy. It seems mind boggling that such an amazing, wise and insightful man as Emanuel Swedenborg could remain such an obscure reference in today's modern world.

The most interesting fact is that Emanuel Swedenborg did not consider any of his scientific contributions to be his finest achievements. He felt that the writings he left us on the nature of the Spiritual world and its relationship to the physical world was his greatest and most meaningful work. Swedenborg began his Spiritual writings when he was in his late fifties. For most of his life he had been able to focus and concentrate his attention, entering into a trance-like state. Then, at the age of fifty-six, he said he was given permission to break through into the Spiritual realm, discourse with higher and lower order beings, and observe the infrastructure of Heaven and hell, firsthand. Swedenborg wrote about it as it was given to him, so that we could understand who we are and why we are here. Nice work, if you can find it!

What I find most impressive about Swedenborg's unique brand of wisdom is his forensic breakdown of consciousness itself. And the bottom line is that we do not have consciousness, it is not a possession that we could lose, misplace or have stolen. We *are* consciousness. We do not have love; we *are* love. Love and awareness are indivisible; therefore you are what you love, and you love whatever you give your attention to.

Swedenborg was very big on a few principles: One, only give your attention to what is unlimited - do not love anything limited. Two, make the most of your human experience by choosing to grow beyond any limiting habits of attention, by putting them down here and now, while we can. And three, to remember that you are pure love, and simply forget everything else.

Swedenborg, being the good and loyal resident of Heaven that he was, talked with Angels daily. Many people came to Swedenborg and asked him for information on loved ones that had crossed over — to access valuable information or property. Swedenborg would enter into his trance-like state of concentrated focus and ask the Angels if he had permission to access the requested information. There are many stories referred to as "minor miracles" where Swedenborg would provided the sought after details, as directed by the Angelic community.

My favorite of these "minor miracle" stories is about a letter Swedenborg had received from John Wesley, (founder of the Methodist denomination).

He asked to meet with Swedenborg at the end of April. Swedenborg wrote back that he would love to meet with Wesley, but that he was scheduled to die in the previous month, so they had best move up the suggested meeting time. Swedenborg knew the day and exact time of his crossing over. He was staying at a friend's house, taking a nap, when the maid came in and woke him up. He asked what time it was. The maid told him, "Five o'clock." He simply smiled and said, "It is good" and crossed over for the last time. If I had spent the last twenty-six years of my life getting to know the other side, I am sure I too would announce, "It is good" on my way out.

Swedenborg once said that he remembered overhearing two Angels in Heaven talking about the Earth. They were saying that it was too bad there was so much conflict and intolerance between people of different belief systems. The Angels were saying that is too bad that the people of Earth could not see that every form of Spiritual and religious expression was like a different jewel in the King's treasure. It is sad and disappointing that the diamonds were jealous of the emeralds, and that the sapphires could not embrace the rubies. All the ideologies are really nothing more than different precious stones in the King's crown. There seems to be more value in focusing on the love that we all have in common, rather than defending and investing in the illusion that we are all some how separate and disconnected. Swedenborg may have crossed over more than two hundred years ago, however it seems there are some ideas that survive as timeless, precious and always worthy of our attention.

The Anatomy of Prayer

Know what the difference is between someone who prays in a church and someone who prays in a casino? The person in the casino *really* means it. Oh please God, if I can just:

1). Win one more hand.

2). Break even.

3). Roll a 7.

4). All of the above . . .

I will never gamble again! And I *really* mean it this time.

Whew! All God needs is for another casino to open. I'm sure She has Her hands full with Las Vegas and online Texas Hold 'em alone.

So what *really* is prayer? How is it different from any other quality of thought or communication we give attention to or engage in? Ever look up the word prayer in the dictionary or the thesaurus? You will see a few choice words repeatedly: supplication, petition, request, entreaty. It would seem that when we initially turn to consider the phenomena of prayer, we link it with . . . a wanting, a needing. This in turn implies that a state of lack must pre-exist before the prayer action/motivation can develop.

At the very least there is a critical environment of deficiency that is the fundamental requirement for the basis of all prayer. With this in mind, the pedestrian equation for prayer is this:

need/lack/want + what I can get from God = Prayer (Lucky 7)

Is there something that makes prayer different from any of the other flotsam and jetsam thoughts that float endlessly across our field of attention? Let's start with intention: the intention to direct a specific communication from you to God. Essentially prayer is thought with more focus attached to it…thoughts on steroids. Our equation then becomes

Thoughts + Focus = Prayer (3 Bars on the progressive slots)

Let's pick this apart even further. Is there a difference between a prayer that someone makes at the blackjack table and the prayer someone makes at the bedside of a sick, injured, or dying loved one? Some may argue both bedside and the "green felt" tableside prayer carry the same gravity of life and death magnitude, but anyone shaking a pair of dice, praying that baby gets that new pair of shoes, is most likely lacking in the same quality of sincerity in their supplication. The underlying question is what is the Ruling Love behind that invocation? Is this a short, shoddy affair with prayer that ends the minute the game of chance is over, one that is navigated, constructed, and dominated by a misdirected, unhealthy ego? Or is there something else going on. Is there a deeper, nurturing, cultivating of wisdom, and strengthening of Spirit that is developing? Is the one praying radiating from a core of love, the natural byproduct of touching the face of God?

Ultimately, there is no right way or wrong way to pray, at least not in the way we typically think of right and wrong. The very fact that one wishes to connect and share communion with God is going to outweigh execution of technique. Prayer is not dependent on how well you perform some stupid human trick. The real matter of consequence is: *why do you do it* and is that inspiration invoked and directed from your ego or from your Heart? So relax. Whether you are clutching a rosary or a sandalwood mala; whether you do it on bended knee or with out-stretched arms; whether you chant or burn something in a puja; whether you do it in a hospital or while playing strip poker, God's hearing is unimpaired. Divine Love and Wisdom will still take your call. How deeply and expansively the prayer opens you up inwardly is what prayer is really about.

It is not that praying to win in Vegas is wrong and praying for a loftier outcome is right. It is about authentically connecting the person praying with Prime Source as One and about what aspect of yourself you are offering up in that relationship. The ego is a shallow container, already filled to the brim with its own charged agenda. The Heart is infinitely expansive. The Heart is naturally and organically designed to unify human and Divine consciousness. The question is not what do you pray for or how you do it, but rather from what internal place does the communication originate?

I am not here to judge who makes a prayer that is myopically driven by an imbalanced, self-absorbed nature and whose prayers make it to Heaven's five star most honored list. This is about regarding and relating to prayer from a place that values it as a powerful and transformational communication that aligns us with our true nature, which is infinite and unlimited Divine

Love and Wisdom. This is about embracing, integrating, and owning a relationship that is the very substance and fabric of miracles and the miraculous. And maybe that is what happens for you when you roll a seven with your life on the Pass line.

All that is important here is that when opening a dialogue about prayer, take a moment to consider whether we are reaching out from our Heart or if our ego is of paramount importance. Remain open-Hearted and open-minded enough to know that prayer is more than emailing a wish list to the big Spiritual Santa Claus in the sky. If your prayer for an iPhone has not been answered, then try faxing in your request. Real prayer contains the opportunity to profoundly change who and what we are; it is the seed from which liberation and enlightenment are sown, by opening ourselves up to a conduit that potentially aligns our free will with God's. Now *that* is worth betting on. Come on . . . . . . Spiritual 7!

TAKE YOUR PICK!

An Interview with Vaishāli

By Stephen McCrory

Can you tell me more about the concept of humanity as spiritual beings in a physical reality that you talk about in your new book "You Are What You Love"?

The earth was created as a place where spiritual creatures could come and practice giving their attention to the truth, to the exclusion of everything else. As mystic Emanuel Swedenborg refers to it, the earth is the place where the limited, the physical, and what lives in duality shows up. We as Spiritual beings are beyond the physical, the limited and duality. What we really are does not even show up here. Only the stuff we are here to get over shows up here, so that we can practice realizing ourselves as beyond it, in an arena we cannot fake.

You are what you love, and you love whatever you are giving your attention to. In the spiritual world, Swedenborg says, we cannot learn that lesson, as well as loyalty to unconditional love and acceptance, as thoroughly as we can on earth in a body, where we have to feel the consequences of what we give our attention to. A feeling body is the "keep it real" arena.

In your book you speak about this wave of awareness. How is it relevant to our daily lives and the choices we make?

The wave is a Swedenborg metaphor for human consciousness. The wave is simply meant as an imaginary vehicle, a method for visualizing something as vast and infinite as consciousness itself.

Through the wave metaphor we can perform a visual forensic examination of consciousness itself. For example, this image allows us to see how superficial what we think and believe is, as it corresponds to the white frothy foam that merely surfs along the surface of the wave. The crest, or top 10% of the wave, corresponds to the part of our consciousness that we live in, what we are aware of.

We came here to practice, in our everyday life, expanding how we define and see ourselves. In other words, the truth is, the wave and the ocean are authentically one. However, most of us only consciously reside in the top 10% of the wave; we have not yet realized our indivisibility with Prime Source. We have not claimed that we do not have God consciousness, we *are* God consciousness. Where we identify ourselves as residing only in the crest, only as the wave, Swedenborg is illustrating the bigger picture. The relevance is in the Gestalt that connects us, as one with Prime Source, in the exact same way the wave is one with the ocean.

If one isn't fully awakened, how can they begin the discernment process of ultimate truth and ultimate lies?
This is why the earth was created: to give spiritual creatures an arena to practice their powers of discernment in. If you find yourself on the earth, in a body, heaven has already set you up with everything you need. How do we begin the discernment process? The same way that we get to Carnegie Hall: practice, practice! You see, that is the gift behind suffering on the earth! Suffering is the wake up call! Suffering keeps our ass honest! Suffering gets our attention! Suffering is the "keep it real" gift. When we give our attention to ultimate lies the suffering increases. When we give our attention to Ultimate Truth the suf-

fering decreases. All sacred traditions state that when we get tired of inflicting suffering upon ourselves with our attention, then and only then will we stop.

Suffering has a purpose. . . . it jump-starts the discernment process!

In your book you talk about how one can either expand into truth or contract back into illusion. How does this work?
This all goes back to: you are what you love and you love whatever you are giving your attention to. No one can be expanding into the truth that they do not have love, value and power, they ARE IT, and at the same time be contracting into a story that it is going to work out for everyone else on the planet but them. We are either building a monument to heaven's truth with our trust in life and love, or we are contracting back into the illusion of unsupported and separated from love by worrying, criticizing ourselves and others, and by seeing only the most negative of outcomes. We are either growing in the light of a higher truth, or we are stagnating in the blindness created by the ego's agenda.

With the discovery of the Indigo and Crystalline children and their heightened awareness, how can a parent guide their children to ask their heart for their truth not their brain . . . especially when the majority of schools and society as a whole tends to teach otherwise?
Well, it is not just school that teaches them otherwise; there is a systemic cultural pressure to use the brain, not the heart. Society in general praises people for thinking their way through life, not feeling their way through it. We all know the "feeling place" and we all know how our intellects can rationalize away anything. We all know how we can think one thing yet feel another.

Parents can remind their children that they have the capacity to drop into their hearts and allow the feeling intelligence to guide them. When children are learning the needs of others, parents can guide them by asking their children, "How would you feel if someone threw a rock at you and called you a 'freak'?" or whatever the situation requires. Parents can support their children in setting their internal compass to point to what is honest and real in the feeling world, because, as Swedenborg points out, what we feel in our hearts is our highest intelligence.

In your book You Are What You Love, you talk about perception as being the magic carpet ride that either elevates us to heaven or plummets us into hell. How can one change their negative perceptions, when they believe that they are accurate and fixed?

One of the major points I am making in the book is the value of letting go of any and all belief systems. Does anyone on this planet know what reality is? As Lilly Tomlin says, "it is nothing more than a collective hunch." In other words, if you do not know what reality is, what are you doing forming a belief system around it? If you do not know what reality is, then practice showing up from an open and innocent heart, and let reality tell you something about its self-evident nature. Then, when you have that one down, you can move on to the next level of mastery. Just remember spiritual truth says that you have to live according to what you love . . . so choose wisely.

How does one begin shifting their perceptions when they are in the habit of operating from years of negative conditioning?

Honesty is essential. If what you are doing is not working for you, meaning it does not support you in a relationship with unconditional happiness and a meaningful existence, then let it go!

The truth is we are all brainwashed. If what you have brainwashed yourself with is not empowering your spiritual identity - that you do not have love you ARE love — then program yourself with an alignment that does.

Again, this is where suffering is designed to be your teacher. If the negativity is recreating suffering in your life, it is nature's way of saying, "put the negativity down, step away from the perceptual weapon, and no one will get hurt."

Only you can realize that you are a timeless, immortal being. Years of negative conditioning are nothing; you are beyond time and the grasp of its limitations.

How does a person begin the process of surrendering and "Waking Up" when fear, pain and negative patterns are keeping one asleep in the disease of duality?
The suffering is not what keeps anyone asleep. Suffering is the Divine design to let you know, in no uncertain terms, that you are surrendering your attention to something outside of heaven. Remaining loyal to the suffering, defending your relationship with limitation, that is what keeps one asleep.

Choosing to remain in bed with familiar fears, rather than face the uncertainty of learning by giving attention to truth, is what keeps anyone asleep at the wheel.

When one surrenders their fears can they then master the human experience?
That is why I wrote the book. This type of authentic probing lies outside of our culture's love for sound bites, fast food and instant gratification. This question, in order to answer it honestly,

requires giving it its multifaceted due. But the most concise way it can be said is this: realize that you are what you love, and you love whatever you are giving your attention to. You came here to practice giving your attention to the truth, to the exclusion of everything else, no matter what the world throws at you. Unconditional conscious alignment with the truth is mastery at its finest.

What revelation would you like the readers or listener of You Are What You Love to walk away with?
Identify with pure love and nothing else, no matter what the world throws at you, because when you do, Heaven is where you will live, unconditionally!

Section 5 ~ Holistic Living

Mind Body Health

Most people think that their inner dialog, their internal running motor mouth, goes no further than the privacy of their own thoughts. According to the Eastern sciences of self-healing — Eastern Indian Ayurveda, Tibetan Ayurveda, and Chinese Medicine — that notion is a dangerously myopic viewpoint. It does not consider the more important aspects of the human experience. Unlike Las Vegas, what goes on inside of us, does not stay inside of us. What we give our attention to has tremendous power in our lives, and it is not limited to residing simply within the confines of our white and grey matter. When we give our attention to thinking that we are unacceptable or unlovable, our emotional body responds to that inner narrative with depression, unhappiness and low self-esteem. Or, when we acknowledge ourselves as capable, wise and deeply blessed with much to be grateful for, our emotional body responds with confidence, self-assurance and contentment. The energy of our thoughts has an effect upon how we feel about ourselves, others and life. It should come as no surprise to discover that nothing else, in or around us, lives in a vacuum either. According to the Eastern philosophies, our bodies and the living things around us take many cues from what we are giving our attention to. It would seem that what we have been experiencing as a private, singular, solitary event has greater, more far reaching consequences than we here in the West are accustomed to considering.

Let's start with the body. Like our emotional sensitivity, the body takes direction and organizes itself around what we think. When we give attention to an inner narrative that describes life as an un-supported, stressful event that will never provide us with what we need, our spleen and pancreas suffer as a response to the energy of that thought. When we tell ourselves how much we dislike some-one or something, when we feed our mental fire with thoughts that produce anger, resentment or frustration, that self-talk affects the liver and gall bladder with an unbalancing result. Our body's inner wisdom about how to function and achieve balance is inti-mately linked to, and driven by, what we are telling ourselves. The energy of our thoughts, our inner dialog, permeates every tissue, every cell, every atom of our bodies. Imagine the body as a mir-ror, reflecting back to us what we are doing with our awareness. According to these Eastern healing sciences, that *is* exactly what is going on. The body is neutral; the mind is not. The body orga-nizes its intelligence by the charge our thoughts create.

If you give your attention to communicating to the body that you love it, trust it, know it can heal itself, the body will respond to the energy of that loving attention as the blueprint for what to do next. Conversely, if you organize your attention to think-ing about an illness as yours — you keep referring to a condition as "my cancer" — the body will have a harder time resolving the disease, because it overheard your thoughts define it as belonging to you. When thoughts label something as "yours" the energy of that inner dialog creates a cul-de-sac within the mind and body that holds onto whatever you have attached a sense of "owner-ship" to. If this self-talk is applied to "my stress," "my arthritis," "my big butt" the body will go out of its way to maintain that self-defined reality for you, because it is under the impression you want it, by virtue of your claiming and owning it as "self".

Furthermore, Ayurveda says that when you eat something, the body will respond to what you are thinking about the food while digesting the meal. Your attitude about what you consume directly affects digestion, assimilation and release of the waste portion of what you ingest. Love is the most powerful force in the Universe. According to Eastern philosophies, when you eat something and you give it loving attention, you empower your body with that transformative intelligence. So if you know you are going to a summer outdoor party, and you know you are going to eat traditional "picnic" cuisine, put love in your heart for what you are about to enjoy, *before* putting that barbecue on your plate. Then, when you eat that double-meat cheeseburger, savor lovingly every mouthful, every morsel. Tell your body how much you totally love the union with this food. When you eat your food with a loving, accepting inner dialog, your body knows what nutrients to take to the deeper tissues and what waste to take to the back door. Ayurvedic medicine says that when you eat something and then think, "Oh, I should not have eaten that!" the energy of that thought confuses the body, and it will contract around the toxins instead of purging them, without attachment or delay.

These Eastern systems say that what you give your attention to while buying, preparing and cooking your food also has a profound effect upon the food itself. When you buy your food with an attitude of gratitude, that energy literally goes into the food. When you prepare your meal and cook it with attention to how much you love this meal, how much you love your life, *that* energy goes into the food as well. Then, when you eat that food, the energy you have infused into the food via your awareness feeds and nourishes not only your physical and emotional bodies, it also sustains your consciousness itself. You are literally feeding your awareness with the quality of consciousness that has permeated your food. This is why it is essential not to cook or eat while you are embroiled in a deeply negative mental/emotional mindset. It is also important to eat at restaurants where the food is lovingly prepared by people who adore what they do, who are grateful for the opportunity to express their devotion in a creative culinary language. When you eat a meal prepared by someone who is angry with their lives, or their minimum wage job, you are literally eating that mental/emotional garbage. That's what I call "junk" food.

Isn't it ironic that here in the West we focus so much on what we are eating and not what is eating us. We obsess over calories and carbs, but never once consider what toxic attitude we are pouring over our food. We think of our meal as only consisting of what we put in our mouths, and not what we have placed in our hearts. We have so compartmentalized everything, that we have lost touch with the power of loving attention and thoughts to unify, heal and bring the integrity of wholeness back into our lives. Understanding that what we give our attention to has *no* boundaries, is the foundation of a life worth living. Choosing wisely the inner self-talk we indulge in is how we feed, heal, sustain and liberate ourselves. Embracing the gift of free will to surrender our attention to what is unlimited and life enhancing is what the journey of life is all about. And remember, the old adage is not necessarily correct: You *can* make chicken salad out of chicken shit. Only your mind knows the recipe.

SALON DE LIMITING THOUGHTS

Food for Thought

*M*ost people think of the digestive process as something limited to the foods and liquids that we stuff into our cake holes daily. However, digestion is best understood as a metaphor for life. (Get used to this metaphor idea, as I am going to keep force-feeding this down your cake hole too.) According to Eastern systems of self-healing, our entire body is an aggregate of different types of digestive intelligences. For example, our eyes digest light waves, so that we can make perceptual sense of our world. Our ears digest sound waves so that we may enjoy our favorite music, (or get indigestion from listening to our windows vibrate from the secondhand rap blaring from a car three blocks away). When we touch one another, our hands digest intimate contact through the tactile feeling feedback system. There is a reason for this conglomerate of digestive efforts. And that is because, as Eastern philosophies say, everything we encounter *is* a form of food; Divine Love and Wisdom has accessorized our human experience with a myriad of assorted digestive skills, so that we might get the most from the nurturing sustenance of life as it is offered to us in its entirety. We are literally digesting our lives.

What digesting your life means, in practical everyday terms, is that every thought, feeling, experience, emotion, etc. that touches our lives, *is* a form of food (since "Man does not live by bread alone"). So let's eat! The first thing we have to be able to do with our *food* is . . . we have to be able to swallow it. Then we need to be able to stomach it. Once we've got it down, we need to pull from these forms of food what enhances us, makes us stronger, wiser, more loving, healthier, balanced people. Finally, we need to be able to let the rest go - to recognize and release the waste in our lives, for what it is.

Now that we have the food part down, let's move on to the main course, the meaty metaphor. The Eastern self-healing philosophies really want you to understand that your thoughts, emotions, perceptions and experiences travel through your digestive tract in the identical fashion as the physical food you eat . . . because *it is* a form of food — a non-physical form of food. If you take something in, mentally or emotionally, and you do not release whatever part of that process contains the waste, the useless, the crap, then you are still carrying that around in your body, and you will continue to do so, until you take it to your metaphorical poop chute and let it go!

So, how much of what we give our attention to, and how much of what we feel about life, can we really swallow, stomach, and convert into life sustaining energy?? Metaphorically speaking, some things can be really *hard to swallow,* and even harder to **stomach**.

Do we ever consider, in our movement through life, if there is anything useful in what we take in, that our bodies – physically, emotionally or energetically – can assimilate, or do we just ingest whatever is put in front of us? Are we simply eating crap, thinking there is something of value in it for us? Well, we must be. Isn't that where the phrase "sh*t eating grin" comes from? Maybe if we use some seasoning, and disguise the taste, our bodies won't notice. Ha! Think again. If what we give our attention to is limiting, then there's nothing there that is useful for us. So how do we assure there is *value* in the food we eat? And, if we do become bloated and constipated by overindulgence in toxic waste, how do we find the emotional, psychological, experiential and perceptual ex-lax needed to *inspire* us to let go of our crap? This is the toughest part of the entire human experience — recognizing the useless in our lives and discarding it completely, instead of clinging to it, thinking it has some place or value. So how do we do it? How do we get rid of what is not serving to us and move on?

We do it with our *awareness*. When we find ourselves giving our attention to worry, or to some other inner dialogue about how we do not have enough time, love, money or opportunity, do we ever question *that* food? Do we consider its nutrient to waste ratio, or do we just shove it down the old cake hole like a 99¢ taco? Do we stop and ask ourselves, "Is that really what we want to feed ourselves? Did we come to planet Earth and take a body just so we could swallow that garbage?" What is the Divine plan behind feeding ourselves a daily critical diet of "didn't do it right" and "not good enough" tasteless morsels? Bet you can't eat just one! In other words, how much of the time, when we find ourselves giving our attention to limiting things, do we *realize* we are actually feeding ourselves refuse, and how much of the time are we just mindlessly taking it in as something that has value and legitimate meaning in our lives?

The best way not to partake of the crap, the doodoo du jour, is to ask yourself if what you are giving your attention to looks, sounds, tastes, smells or feels limiting. If the answer is, "Hell, yes! The thought that you will never be happy, and that nothing is going to work out for you is across-the-board limiting," then the healthy digestive answer would be to take that item off your diet. Do not give what is limiting your attention, unless you want to feed yourself noxious, meaningless, *mean cuisine.* If you want to poison your body with what is pointless, bon appetit! This digestive metaphor thing brings a whole new meaning to "junk food". (It's not just the nitrites in hot dogs any more.)

If you find yourself consuming mass quantities of negativity, in the same way that the Coneheads consumed beer and chips, there is a digestive remedy. Stop! Recognize what you are giving your attention to, and choose something else. Giving your attention to what is unlimiting will always purify the poison. When you give your attention to what is unlimiting, the emotional, mental and physical bodies will immediately recognize what needs to be discarded from what needs to be taken deeper to sustain life.

Ever wonder why the body holds on to some forms of waste and toxins and releases others? What's up with that? Ever wonder why some people can eat foods that make others ill? How can *that* happen? The truth is, *digestion is a metaphor*, as well as a physically based reality. How well our body is (or is not) digesting food is a reflection of the bigger picture: how well are we digesting our lives — our thoughts, emotions, experiences and perceptions. What toxic energy are we holding onto perceptually and emotionally, that our bodies, by way of dis-ease and illness, are reflecting back to us? What are we inviting ourselves to let go of internally - both psychologically, as well as physiologically? What is it that our bodies cannot separate from, because the mind has formed an attachment to? In the flow of life, what are we holding onto, because we do not understand what is enhancing and what is diminishing? What are we eating, versus what is eating us? What are we mindlessly consuming, and what are we consuming mindfully?

We can become aware of what our unconscious issues are by examining what the digestive process is reflecting back to us, forcing us to *feel* the limitation of it. Where in your body do you feel you have stuffed something you do not trust mentally or emotionally? Is it in your gut? Could it be . . . because *it is* in your gut! Remember, digestion is a metaphor for how well are we swallowing, stomaching and nurturing our human experience with all of the universal food we consume on a moment-to-moment basis.

In the West, we define digestion as starting with the mouth, chewing and mixing with saliva, then swallowing. The Eastern systems of self-healing find that laughable. The Eastern philosophies say that digestion starts when you *see* the food, when you *smell* the food, when you *touch* it with your fingers; the cake hole is the last guy to get on the digestive bus, not the first. How many times have you told yourself while driving home that you were not hungry, only to open the front door, smell dinner cooking, and have your stomach start to rumble? How many times have you driven to the grocery store when you were not hungry, then, as you walked up and down the isles, touching the fruits and veggies, you found yourself ready to eat everything in your shopping cart, along with all the impulse items at checkout? And let's not forget about Pavlov's dogs! How many of you were not hungry until you heard the dinner bell – as in the sound of bacon frying, bagels popping out of a toaster, dinner plates clanging? You can clearly see from this part of the metaphor, that digestion starts not only at a perceptual level, but also at any level that involves the five senses. That is why digestion of life happens when you give something your attention, when you touch something, or when you experience something with any or all of your senses. You start digesting your day even before you smell the coffee brewing. Speaking of smelling the coffee, have you ever noticed that the olfactory part of digestion is always the most satisfying? How many times have you walked into an establishment, smelled freshly ground coffee that made your legs weak, only to find it tasted so bitter you couldn't drink it?

In the same way that the brain digests our thoughts and beliefs, and the nervous system digests what we feel on a tactile level, our internal organs, in addition to having a physical food-related function, also digest our emotions. According the Eastern system of medicine, each internal organ has a specific emotional food digestive/transformative process. For example, the spleen, stomach and pancreas digest anxiety, worry, and nervousness. That is why we get "butterflies" in the stomach when anticipating or perceiving something involving stress. The liver and gall-bladder take on anger, rage, envy, and frustration. The heart and small intestines digest impatience, and the kidneys and bladder deal with fear and terror. The lungs and large intestines have the task of breaking down loneliness, sadness and grief, as well as low self-esteem issues and feeling of worthlessness.

This process is how one can begin to unravel the unresolved unconscious issues in life. Looking at the body's health, what organs are stressed? Where is the weak link in the chain? It is there you will discover the undigested systemic problems in your life. No wonder Socrates felt the unexamined life was not worth living. Why would anyone want to live a life filled with unconsciously driven pain and undigested emotional angst? After all, if you wanted to be treated like that you would just go see your family! (Oops. I guess that's part of my unresolved unconscious issues coming up as *acid* reflux.)

However, digestion does not stop there. To the Eastern systems of self-healing, respiration is one of our most profound digestive functions. Yes, that's right; you read that correctly. ***Breathing*** is a powerful form of digestion. I know, you are all thinking . . . breathing . . . whaaat? How can that be? The breath goes in, the breath goes out. What could be so complicated about that? Well, for starters, most of you out there are not breathing the way your body was designed! Breathing is how we digest our emotions. How you breathe determines whether or not you are holding onto emotional toxic energy in your life or releasing it. Ever watch how babies breathe? Their lower abdomen expands on the inhale, their chest moves last and moves the least. When a baby has an emotional moment, they experience it, then they let it go. A baby can go from crying to laughing in 60 seconds flat. Babies digest the emotion, experience, and perception, release it, and find themselves available for the next round. Ever examine how you are breathing? I bet dollars to donuts, no food pun intended (and no disrespect to Homer Simpson), that your chest moves first and most dramatically, and your lower abdomen moves last and least. Do you ever experience something and cannot seem to let it go? You find yourself internally reliving that charge over and over again? How you breathe is playing a part in this digestive Groundhog Day scenario.

If babies are breathing the way we are designed to, then how come we start out functioning correctly, and end up all ass backwards? The answer: the diaphragm. The diaphragm is a large muscle that literally cuts your body into two halves at the lower rib cage. When the diaphragm moves down on the inhale, the emotional digestive mechanism is turned on, just as we see in babies. When the diaphragm moves up on the inhale, the exact opposite to how we are designed to function, it causes the chest to move first, and the emotional digestive mechanism gets turned off.

Babies breathe the way we are all designed to, because they do not give their attention to limiting ideas about themselves or life. Babies gradually learn to do that from the world around them. Babies watch the people around them not digesting their lives. Babies witness others not breathing correctly. Babies watch, learn and mimic; they take it all in, for better or worse. As the child learns to give their attention to limited things, as they progress in repressing their emotions and fears, the diaphragm gradually inverts its natural movement and, voila, the accumulation of undigested life begins!

This is one of the many reasons Eastern forms of meditation have you focus on the breath. Breathing only happens in the present moment; you cannot breathe in the past, or breathe in the future. Breathing correctly and deeply detoxifies you physically, emotionally, psychologically and Spiritually. And you thought breathing was a no brainier! Well guess what? Correct breathing is not just for babies anymore!

Digesting our lives involves a deep connection to our awareness. What are we giving our attention to? Is it something unlimited, something we can swallow and stomach on every level? Or are we feeding ourselves unpasteurized, intellectual and perceptual toxins? Consider what you feed yourself. Consider and weigh every aspect and implication of that question. Examine if you are breathing completely and deeply enough to activate your emotional digestive system, or if your breathing never progresses beyond a shallow chest involvement, stopping at the heart, creating emotional denial and suppression - truly a superficial digestive engagement.

So the next time your find yourself hungry for any aspect of life, take a deep breath; focus on what is most life enhancing; only eat at fine dining establishments, and be sure and read the menu first. Assess your choices, and most of all ... try not to eat what's sitting out back in the garbage cans. But if you do, learn to let it go! Happy releasing!

Consciousness:
The Ultimate Digestive Aid

*D*eepak Chopra said it best when he stated that the body is constantly eavesdropping in on what we think about it, and what we are giving our attention to. This only makes sense, since our awareness existed long before we inherited this physical packaging from our parents, and it will exist long after we have outgrown a need for it. Our bodies are inherently neutral. The charge that our consciousness holds, that direction of intention and perspective, will ultimately determine how our bodies respond to every stimulus we encounter, both internally and externally.

All of the internal organs of the body are designed to digest the emotional food of our lives, in the same way that they digest the physical food of our lives. The liver is neutral to traffic, taxes, in-laws and cellulite; but our mind and our thought process, however, are not. Once we focus our awareness on the caustic and abrasive nature of what we label mildly irritating to downright uncontrollably offensive, the emotions of anger, frustration, and rage will move through the nervous system and through the digestive tract. Once this particular emotional food reaches the liver, the liver's job is to break it down, pull from it what we need, and move the rest out for the identifiable waste that it is. This is accomplished much in the same way that the liver produces bile, stored in the gall bladder, for release in breaking down and digesting lipids and fats. How does the liver know we have swallowed a mouthful of anger? It knows, because like the rest of our body, it is listening to our consciousness. It is following the charge created in the mind.

There is no separation between consciousness and the emotional and physical processes of our lives. With this in mind, a science was developed to successfully balance the execution of our everyday lives. It is called Ayurveda, which literally translates to "the science of everyday life." And this is why Ayurveda emphasizes establishing routine in our everyday life: to carry out healthy habits with a focus of attention that is most serving to us, without distraction from what keeps us balanced, happy and self-realizing. In the thousands of years the wisdom of Ayurveda has been on the planet, the distractions may have changed, but the message remains the same.

Training the focus of our awareness and flow of consciousness is the entire purpose behind meditation. However the support of this attention discipline should not be limited to our quiet time practice. The benefit of the Ayurvedic routine is that it transforms our everyday life flow into a training ground of refining the movement of consciousness and intention setting. Due to the pervasive nature of our thoughts, Ayurveda suggests a routine of focusing on how grateful we are for our food and how we give our bodies permission to be deeply nourished, strengthened and healed by what we consume. That mindset, the intention that the body is eavesdropping in on, is sustained in every step of that relationship: from the trip to the store where you first see and touch your food, through the preparation process of cleaning, chopping and cooking the food. According to Ayurveda the first step of digestion happens not in the mouth, but when you first see and touch your food, even if it is just looking at a picture of it in a menu or visualizing it. That is why Homer Simpson salivates the minute he thinks about donuts…ummm donuts. In our modern culinary world of freezer to microwave cuisine, we frequently skip this step of pre-programming the body to our highest intention. For most of us the thought of even remotely considering gratitude comes in a flash, just before we devour our food, and is usually distracted by our fixation on the food itself. No wonder we feel no emotional or physiological satisfaction from what we eat. We have not routinely trained the body to expect and to receive that "quality" of food.

Listening to music that inspires and lifts our Spirit while we prepare our meal is a nice routine helper. It supports us in maintaining awareness that whatever we give our attention to while organizing and eating our meal is what we will energetically be consuming *with* our meal. Avoid watching 24-hour news channels or other related programs that focus on fear-based messages and distract you from feeling safe and nurtured in the present moment.

Raising our digestive fire before eating can be very important and essential in giving our body the boost it needs to extract what is most life sustaining from our food. Ayurveda suggests lighting a candle when you are preparing and enjoying your food. When our attention goes out to lighting and watching the fire on the candle, that action triggers the enhancement of our inner digestive fire or agni. Once again, what we are doing with our attention is the magic and power in our lives. Lighting a candle is a simple and lovely way to bring your focus back to the present moment and the action at hand. It is illuminating and warming. Fire is naturally hypnotic as well. That is why we easily find ourselves gazing into a fire whether it is on our stovetop or in the living room fireplace.

Consciousness is eternal. We bring it with us when we come to the Earth, and as a parting gift from Prime Source, we take to with us when we leave. The purpose of life in a body on the Earth is to practice and realize right relationship with consciousness. It is a practice that never goes out of style. It is a relationship that we never outgrow. And, there is no time like the present to make your mind your friend. Your physical and emotional bodies will thank you for it.

7 Simple Tips To Improving Digestion

Our digestive system is the cornerstone of all the body's health and strength - emotional, mental, as well as physical. These are simple Ayurvedic tips to optimize your digestive system.

1. Do not eat if you do no feel hungry. Feeling hungry is your body's way of letting you know that the digestive system is primed and ready to work. Eating when you are not hungry, out of boredom or habit, stresses the digestive system to start working before it is ready to do so.

2. Your digestive fire is similar to any kind of fire. Kindling and stoking it brings the flame higher. The higher the flame the more efficient the process. Have a glass of wine with your meal. Alcohol is extremely fire proving, it is like pouring gas on the fire. Another way is to cut raw ginger root into thin slices, squeeze some lime juice and dust lightly with sea salt. Eat this 10 to 15 minutes before the meal.

3. Cup your two hands together. That unit of measure correlates to the size of your stomach, and

how much you should be ingesting at any meal. Optimally we should be filling the stomach as follows: one third is food, one third is liquid and the other third is space. This gives the stomach room for mixing and churning.

4. Wait two and half hours between meals and snacking. Your digestive tract needs about two and half hours to complete a digestive cycle after eating. Consuming foods faster than that stresses the digestive system to begin another cycle before it is ready.

5. Poor food combining causes toxins to build up in the digestive tract. For example, fruits are mostly water and should not be mixed with dairy, grains, meat or vegetables. Fruits like strawberries and melons are "eat it alone or leave it alone" fruits. There are more rules for healthy food combining too numerous to list here.

6. Do not consume cold food or beverages. Your stomach is like a pot on the stove. You want it to be hot so it can cook and properly break down the food. Consuming something cold stresses the digestive system to energetically bring up the heat.

7. The digestive system loves soups and stews. When you mix foods and cook them together on your stovetop, that allows the foods to work out their chi or energy differences. It is better to work out that energy battle on your stovetop than in your body.

Contemplating the Navel

*I*t all started when I was in my mid-twenties, with a small pain in the abdomen. Little did I know how this little pain would force me to make big changes in my life. The pain seemed concentrated in three points around the right ovary. It became most acute when I would bend over. The mystery pains gradually grew until they were bothering me all the time, regardless of posture or position. I did what most people would do when seeking to address something health related: I made an appointment with my doctor. He was a better listener than most doctors and took the time to do a physical examination. While examining the pelvis, he found that merely touching that area was enough to produce pain, so we agree to proceed with non-invasive testing. That started off simple enough: leaving bodily fluid in a cup, taking a blood sample, or an ultra sound test. (For you guys, it would be the equivalent of "turn your head and cough".) Everything we tried was inconclusive.

Over the course of a year, the pain spread down the right leg and across the lower back. I pretty much just dragged my right leg around. My abdomen slowly swelled until there was a constant state of discomforting distention. My skin turned a pasty shade of gray with tiny bumps, the greatest concentration being on my back. I looked like a cross between Quasimodo and a heroin addict. Looking back on it now, I can understand that my skin looked this way because it was the only organ still detoxifying my entire body. I lived with a hot water bottle stuffed down my pants. It was the only thing I could do to help alleviate the non-stop pain that plagued the lower body. Due to my declining condition, my doctor suggested we try exploratory surgery. The best way to know what was going on would be to look directly into the body. The way I felt, I agreed.

My doctor and I discussed best and worst possible scenarios so that I would be prepared. The worst case would be that they might have to start removing organs. We still suspected if there was a problem, (if you could have seen me, that would have been a no-brainer) it would be centered on the reproduction organs. I was perfectly fine living without some or all of my reproductive organs . . . I didn't need them to live. But I only had one heart or liver, and those I did need.

I clearly remember the moment I regained consciousness in the recovery room. My doctor would not make eye contact with me, and I was thinking, "This can't be good." He said, "I have some good news and some bad news. I'll start with the good news. We did not take anything out; you still have all your organs." "Great!" I was thinking, "What could possibly be the bad news?" "The bad news is that every organ from your stomach to your colon is in crisis." He then took a quarter out of his pocket. "Your liver and small intestine are the worst. I could flip this quarter to determine which organ will shut down first, but most likely you are going to die from either the liver or small intestine shutting down, and I do not know why."

My doctor referred me to a digestive specialist who acted like he was God's gift to the medical profession. Maybe it was due to his years of working with the lower GI tract, that he treated everyone like they were a piece of sh*t. He came into the room, looked at the chart, and said, "I am going to run a bunch of invasive tests, and then be prepared for me to tell you that there is nothing wrong with you." I was shocked! This man had not even examined me, yet he was dismissing me out of hand. "You *have* seen the surgery notes from my other doctor, haven't you? How can you say that?" I asked completely stunned by his insensitivity, arrogance, and confrontational attitude. "Is your other doctor a digestive specialist?" he spat out in a very aggressive and hostile tone. "No, he isn't," I answered. "I'd be surprised if your other doctor even knows where your liver *is*!" He snapped with no deference to cordiality or even superficial professional courtesy. He then proceeded to load up my arms with bags, hoses and bottles of fluid, told me to reschedule, and shoved me out the door.

Looking back on it now, I can see that this specialist, unintentionally, did me the biggest favor of my life. I remember walking over to the nearest trashcan, opening my arms, and dumping all the medical paraphernalia unceremoniously into the garbage. I walked away thinking, "I am going to have to figure this out myself. These people do not know what they are doing." I am not advising other people to abandon their doctors, but for me it was the right choice. And it changed my life forever.

I had for the most part accepted the terminal diagnosis, but as long as I was still alive, I wanted to try and minimize the excruciating pain I was in all the time. The pain of having your organs rotting inside your body is horrible; it would make you want to jump off a building. (Good thing I lived on the first floor at this time in my life.) I would sometimes lay in bed in agony, unable to move, and just cry and whimper for hours. I had to train my roommates to be neutral to my suffering, as I could not deal with their reactions and my situation at the same time. Besides I knew their panicking was not going to do anything but increase my already 'through the ceiling' stress level.

I heard about a rare Chinese form of internal organ massage called Chi Nei Tsang, and decided to try it. Fortunately for me, I stumbled into the office of Gilles Marin, the foremost master in this technique. He worked on me for about ten minutes and then said, "Okay, I am going to tell you what is wrong with you. I'm warning you now it is going to be extremely hard for you to hear, because you have been diagnosed as terminal and been through so much pain for so long. The problem with you is that you are not breathing correctly." My first thought was, "What an asshole! If it was my breathing, I would have been dead long before now."

Gilles explained that breathing is how we digest our emotions, thoughts and experiences, as well as supply oxygen to the body. "You have absorbed as much fear as a person can, and still be alive, but just barely alive." It is true my childhood was a succession of one highly traumatizing event after another. It was also true that after the exploratory surgery, I discovered that my live-in boyfriend was sleeping with the women who were supposed to be my good friends. The widespread, deep-seated betrayal was emotionally devastating. I remember thinking that they did not even have the courtesy to wait until I died. How rude can you get! I was also working for my boyfriend's parents, so when we split up, I was advised to find another job. This meant losing my health insurance and trying to find gainful employment while physically suffering from pain that some days would not even let me get out of bed. And worse, I now had a "pre-existing condition" which would preclude me from ever getting health insurance and probably another job. I had wanted to jump off a building to get out of the pain, but instead I inadvertently got thrown under the bus. Ain't life grand! My life was turning into a country western song.

Even withstanding Gilles' accuracy about my history, which he could not possibly have known anything about, the idea that my breathing had anything to do with my present situation was just too foreign for me to accept. "You're not even working where it hurts," I told Gilles when he started back with the massage, just to show him he lacked the correct insight into my case. "I know. It hurts here, here and here," he said, touching the three painful spots around the right ovary that had started this whole wild ride. No doctor had ever been able to make sense of these three spots when they asked me where it hurt. And now, out of nowhere, this guy zeroes in on them without any guidance on my part.

"How did you know that?" I asked completely stunned. Gilles explained, "The diaphragm in the body is designed to move downwards on the inhale. Yours is moving in exactly the opposite direction. Instead of going down, it is coming up. It is pulled up so high in the front of your body it is pinching off your liver meridian, cutting off your liver from desperately needed Chi, life force, energy. Your liver is hanging on by a thread now because the flow of energy has been choked off for so long. The result is the liver and the liver meridian are swollen and in crisis. The liver meridian comes closest to the surface of the skin where the most nerve endings are, and then dives back down here, here and here (those three spots). So that is where you would be experiencing the most pain. When you learn how to breathe correctly and bring the diaphragm back down, the flow of energy will be restored to your liver, and it will come right back, because there is nothing wrong with your liver. Your doctors were right about one thing, however, and that is you will die *if* you do not change how you breathe. But you do not have to die; there is still time. You can reverse this."

In ten minutes this guy explained my pain, how I got it, and what I needed to do to recover fully from it. Modern medicine had my case for over a year without any doctor, including a specialist, offering me any tangible insights or wisdom. I remember thinking that even if this guy is not right, it couldn't hurt me to learn to breathe more efficiently and harmoniously. I shut my mouth, followed Gilles' instructions, and began to focus on what happened when I breathed.

Chi Nei Tsang is designed to be self-administered, so I spent the next several years studying with Gilles. The first year of the recovery process was extremely intense. In addition to retraining the respiration and the actual physical manipulation of the internal organs, an emotional exorcism occurs. The massage is about purging the body of negative emotions and bringing consciousness back to the core of the body. In the human experience, this is precisely where consciousness is designed to be seated. For more than a year, I would have an emotional release exactly twenty-four hours following an appointment with Gilles. You could set your clocks by it. The day of the appointment I would feel great. I could tell I was improving dramatically. Then the next day, I would be an emotional basket case. The fear would just start pouring out of me. I had to make arrangements to stay at home the next day, because I was so scared I literally could not function. I had to let the fear come up and release it, without repressing it again out of habit.

During that first year I also experienced profound changes in the myofacial tissue that surrounds the internal organs. The tissue, responding to years of fear stimuli, had grown very tight and had a death grip around the organs. The combination of the breathing exercises and the emotional releases from organ manipulation caused the tissue to rip loose from the inside out, finally permitting the organs to relax. The sensation of the tissue tearing loose inside the body was a bizarre combination of blinding pain followed by the sweet bliss of relief.

I spent so much time studying this internal organ massage and Chinese Medicine, I decided to become a certified practitioner to help other people regain quality of life as well. I gradually branched out and studied both Eastern Indian Ayurveda and Tibetan Ayurveda. These healing sciences are based on body types. Unlike the Western concept of the body, a mechanistic paradigm that sees all bodies as the same, Eastern systems see every person as unique: a universe unto themselves. And it is imperative that one knows about the various body types, their strengths and weaknesses, in order to understand how to achieve and maintain optimal balance and health. Now that I have this knowledge I find it difficult to see how most people survive our culture without its benefits. I guess the truth is most people don't survive it well.

The heart of the internal organ massage is the navel. That is the window to the health of the body. The ideal navel should be round, symmetrical and flat with a well defined rim, walls and a floor. Any distortions in this ideal round shape are due to stresses and toxins in the internal organs as well as poor or incorrect breathing patterns. The best way to get a good clear reading on the navel is to lie on the back, knees bent and the pelvis tilted slightly forward. Then, with the head resting flat, use a mirror to see what the navel looks like in this "at rest" position. If the head is lifted to see what the abdomen looks like, it will pull on the navel and the reading will not be accurate.

Draw a line with your finger directly from wherever the navel is stretched, pulled or puffy out to the outer perimeter of the body. As you trace outward, your finger will lead you to the organ in question that is causing the navel to be misshapen. The most commonly distorted navels I saw looked like a mail box slot, with the navel looking like a horizontal straight line. This line is pointing to the bottom of the floating ribs and indicates that the floating ribs are not moving in and out on the inhale and exhale. This lack of range of motion in the floating ribs is also going to affect the ascending and descending colon, as well as limit the movement of the diaphragm. When breathing, the movement of the floating ribs acts like a pump and helps pump undigested material up the ascending colon, across the transverse colon, and down the descending colon. The other most common distressed shape I examined was the navel in a slot-like pattern with the straight line pointing vertically. This shape indicates stresses and pulling in both the diaphragm and the lower pelvis. In both of these cases, there was no longer a well-defined rim, walls or floor of the navel; the navel had taken on a horizontal shape or a vertical shape. The healthy and balanced features had been obliterated by the unresolved tensions held within the body.

The navel is a powerful energy center. It is considered to be the recycling center. When starting the massage, the hands should rest right around the rim of the navel. Slowly and gently the fingers begin to make a sinking, spiraling motion downwards, with the stroke always ending towards the center of the navel. It does not matter if you massage in a clock wise or counter clock wise direction, both directions are beneficial. You will instinctually massage in the right direction, without thinking about it. The idea is to move the tension felt by the fingers into the navel, into the recycling center, so that the body can access it and recycle the energy into something more useful. Very gradually, the massaging motion is expanded to an area of about an inch to an inch and a half around the navel. Keep the massaging motion going into the center of the navel. The massaging action is timed with the breath. On the inhale hold the fingers firmly and breath into them, and then on the exhale, tilt the pelvis up a bit more and press into the abdomen. Think of the center of the navel as a vacuum cleaner that is constantly sucking in whatever you sweep into it. Always start as close to the rim of the navel as possible and move whatever tension you feel into the recycling center. Then slowly move outward, sweeping towards the center of the navel, into the energetic vacuum cleaner. There are other more advanced techniques that go deeper into the large intestine and liver, help release the floating ribs, and relax the psoas muscles, but this is the primary technique all others are built on.

You cannot hurt yourself massaging your navel and breathing deeply into the pelvic floor. This action is powerfully detoxifying, so you may feel a bit light-headed at first. That's the toxins moving out. You may also find that your arms tire easily. If you have to stop and rest a bit before continuing, that's fine. This action is cumulative so any amount of time you put into relaxing the navel is beneficial. Twenty minutes a day is a good minimum. It does not matter if it is ten minutes at night and ten minutes in the morning, or two minutes ten times throughout the day. No time is better than another; anytime or any length of time is useful to the body.

I like to do a bit of navel massage just prior to an acupuncture treatment, full body massage or chiropractic adjustment. It helps relax the body and opens it up from the center outwards. If I am experiencing any trouble falling asleep, it is a nice thing to do while waiting to fall asleep, since it sends a message of relaxation to the whole body. In the case of over-eating, navel massage is a great way to support digestion, plus it helps alleviate that over-stuffed and bloated feeling.

We are all designed to breath into our pelvic floor. Ever watch how babies breathe? Their little abdomens move dramatically on the inhale and exhale. Babies breathe the way we are all designed to breathe; they have not yet learned to stuff their emotions. Babies are very "in the moment". One instant they are scared, the next happy and laughing. They digest their emotions fully, and then move on to the next moment. Adults do not do that. We are masters of holding and repressing. Breath also follows consciousness. When we breathe into the pelvic floor, we are consciously residing in the center of our being. As we grow from babies into toddlers, adolescence, then adulthood, we learn to protect ourselves from our emotions. When we move our awareness from our gut up into our heads to insulate ourselves from feeling life too intensely, that action literally hijacks the breath and diaphragm upwards with the flow of consciousness.

Nature does not like a vacuum when we move out, because the undigested emotions, perceptions and experiences that pushed us out, move in. When we learn to bring the breath and awareness back down into the body, these other energies move out. They have to. Our bodies are designed to house our awareness, not fragments of undigested life.

The best way to see, feel and become aware of how much undigested life you carry around is to do the navel massage. When lying on your back, with the knees bent and the pelvis tilted slightly forward, place your palms directly over the navel. Everything under your hands, between the floating ribs and hip bones, is soft tissue. The only bone is the spine in the back. When massaged, soft tissue should just move gently out of the way. To experience this, gently pinch the excess skin on the back of your upper arm. See how the soft tissue easily moves? The soft tissue in your abdomen is no different. It should move the same way. If you are rubbing your navel around the rim, or in the inch to inch and a half zone directly around the rim, and you come in contact with something hard, constrictive, or resistant, ask yourself, "What is this?" It is not the organs. They are soft tissue. It is nothing you ate either. By the time food gets into the lower digestive system, it is a liquid. So what is it? It is undigested life. It is undigested thoughts, feelings, emotions and perceptions. I guess we really are "full of it"!

When I give demonstrations of this work, I actually get on a massage table and let people come by and push on my navel. With not much effort, people can immediately feel my spine from the front. I am committed to digesting the food of life and letting go of the rest for the waste it is. Big or small, physical size does not matter. I am a small-boned person, but I have worked on Gilles, who is a large-boned man, and I can get to his spine from the navel with ease. But then I only learn from the best.

My situation was not a quick fix. It took me years of studying the Eastern systems of self-healing to learn not only how to breathe and digest life effectively, but also what to eat, the proper exercise for my body type, and how to balance the subtle energies that make up the human experience in my everyday life. All in all it took me somewhere between seven and ten years to make a complete recovery. I am much healthier now than most people you will ever meet.

Knowledge of how to manage the human experience is invaluable information regardless of your present health situation. Yes, I did recover from that terminal diagnosis, but ten years later, in my late thirties, I was involved in a car accident. I sustained a life-threatening head injury, and once again the terminal injury diagnosis was bestowed upon me. To this day my doctor will tell you he is amazed I survived that injury. He was convinced it was a death sentence. I know the only reason I survived and, after another decade of healing, have good quality of life, is because of the years I studied these alternative healing sciences. When the car accident happened, I knew how to take responsibility for my own health, well being and ultimate healing.

When I needed that wisdom to save my life, I had it. After the car accident I was not in any position to study anything. I would not have survived if I had to take the time to learn these skills. When the crisis arose, I already knew how to respond, what to do, and when to do it, in order to live. Additionally, I have been able to help others by sharing this priceless, life saving wisdom. There is no downside to understanding the science of everyday life and how to manage the particular body constitution you have been blessed with. Think of these alternative medical sciences as your instruction manual. No one would think of owning a car without knowing what gas to put in it, what oil to use, when to rotate the tires and take it in for service. Our bodies get us around more than our cars, yet most people ignore this valuable information. I guess that's why your mileage may vary. Too bad that extended warranty isn't available for the human body.

My prayer for you would be that you are never faced with over-coming two terminal diagnoses in your lifetime. And if that does find you or a loved one, know you are powerful beyond measure, and there is a vast wealth of life saving wisdom out there for you to discover. In the meantime, be sure to keep your hands where they belong . . . in your navel.

Section 6 ~
Unconventional Wisdom

Out of the Box -
The Only Way to Grow

rom Shākyamuni, the historical Buddha, to Jesus, to
Mohammed, to J. Krishnamurti, the one thing all
great Spiritual teachers have in common is that they
lived, thought and acted outside of the box; the box of their culture, their families, and their peers. We often refer to the freeing of our minds of any limitation as a state of enlightenment.
However, we rarely stop to consider that if we aren't enlightened
beings, it implies that our minds are imprisoned and enslaved by
limitation.

Can you imagine the teachings of these great people if they
limited themselves to the confines of what was acceptable and
agreeable to the mainstream paradigm in which they found
themselves historically dwelling? Can you imagine Shākyamuni
restricting the eight-fold path teachings so that it never strayed
from the "norm"? What if Jesus limited his healing miracles
and personal death transcendence because of what other people
might have thought about him? You gotta figure that people
standing around the tomb of Lazarus most likely thought, "This
Jesus guy's elevator does not go to the top floor." What if Mohammed decided not to write anything down, because no one
else in his family ever did . . . well, so much for Islam.

At some point in every person's life, if they value Spiritual maturity and the process of self-liberation, they must choose life

outside the box. It is the only way to grow. Self-mastery has always been found outside the box of traditional thinking and values. Why? Because true Self is infinite and unlimited, and its authentic exploration would blow 'inside the box' restrictions clear into next week. Without transcending the box of tribal mentality, the best one could ever achieve would be mastery *of* the box . . . nothing more than a fully realized pedestrian existence. With a lack of meaningful self-examination, it is hardly a life worth living.

The real irony about living "inside the box" is that most of us are attracted to it, because it is comfortable. We set up house and make it our permanent mailing address, as we perceive it to be safe. We curb our engagement with life for fear of what other people might say or think about us. We repress creative expressions and behaviors that are outside the "norm." We restrict ourselves to a superficial "people pleasing" level of passionate engagement with life. We spend the bulk of our lives doing what we think we are supposed to do - what is expected of us from family and cultural standards, because we fear letting others down. Out of fear of going against the herd, we spend our entire lives committed to actions and self-imposed limitations we will later regret on our deathbed ~ needless to say a bit late for a "do over."

Consider all the worry, insecurity, guilt and stress that trying to remain a good resident of inside the box thinking creates. Reflect on all the times in your life you told yourself that you could not do something, because growing in an unconventional direction would make those around you uncomfortable, or because you did not want to stick out in a crowd. All the self-squelching and imagination shrinking we do in exchange for tribal/family acceptance. Clinging to the inside of the box costs us so much personally and collectively. So many times I hear people say, "Well, I can't do or dress or communicate in the way I would like to, because other people will be intimidated or have some problem with it." You know, after all, what would the neighbors think! My response has always been, "So what! If other people have a problem with it, that is it not *your* problem. It's theirs; don't make it yours."

It takes so much more time and energy to move forward personally and collectively when shackled to the brilliance diminishing effects of inside the box living. It took humanity centuries to get beyond inside the box thinking. The world is flat; the Sun revolves around the Earth; women should not make as much money as men; there's no such thing as ghosts.

The ideas of great thinkers and contributors of wisdom that have vastly shaped global consciousness have all been pioneers in out of box exploration. Imagine what literature would be like without out of the box voices like Oscar Wilde, Mark Twain, William Shakespeare and Kurt Vonnegut Jr.? I shudder to think what the world would be like if Rosa Parks agreed with the status quo and gave up her seat on the bus every time she was asked to; if Gandhi had remained a lawyer in England; if Martin Luther King Jr. never took his job beyond the walls of a church building; if William Shatner as Captain Kirk had never gone where no man had gone before; or if Rod Serling had never entered the Twilight Zone.

Without an open mind, wisdom cannot penetrate into our perspectives and lives. The first step to real wisdom is a willingness to authentically consider new and different ideas. As always each person must ultimately make up their own mind, but the beginning of any truly free exchange of ideas and information begins with a willingness to consider a different point of view; a different way of doing things, an alternative value system and way of life.

No one ever conquered their fears, embodied their fullest potential, or invented something new by succumbing to the pressures of conformity. What would scientific advancement look like if Albert Einstein waited for his ideas to become mainstream before he introduced E=MC2? The purpose of life is not to perfect one's ability to meet the herd agenda in a vacuum of creative boundary pushing and unbridled daring exploration of possibilities known and unknown. We have to exchange risk taking for comfort when reevaluating the worship of the myopic; the religion of all those loyal to living and thinking inside the box.

Self-knowledge is complete and all-inclusive. Self-realization is so far outside the box that there is no box. If breaking away from tribal influences and restrictions is important to us, then we must be willing to practice being proficient at climbing out of the box. We must be willing to expose ourselves to ideas and views beyond the range of our belief system blinders. We must cultivate an open and honest thirst for the unfamiliar, and for what lies beyond the boundaries of our intellectual, emotional and experiential comfort zones. We must be willing to admit that if we do not know what reality is, it is not in our best interest to act like we do. We must choose to be self-empowering, to untether our perception from the conventional, the middle of the road and the customary. We truly have to be willing to go where no one has gone before, and not just leave that to sci-fi television. We must value investing in human potential and not crumple under the tyranny of mob mentality.

Unconventional wisdom is the herald of authentic excellence. If Edward R. Murrow conformed to traditional standards of journalism, the bar would not have been raised to sheer genius. If Princess Diana acquiesced to the accepted life of a princess in the royal box, many charities would have lost one of the world's great philanthropists. If Lenny Bruce did not take stand-up comedy beyond one-liners and impersonations, George Carlin, Richard Prior and Chris Rock would not have the socially redeeming level of success they presently do. If Joan of Arc and Mother Teresa allowed what was expected of women to influence their lives, history would be missing two very powerful people. If Nostradamus and Edgar Cayce had allowed their religious upbringings to censor their receptivity to Divine Consciousness, the world would have lost two extraordinary prophets. If Emanuel Swedenborg had permitted the narrow-minded and the mainstream to define what was or was not within the realms of human achievement and knowledge, the world would be without a remarkable, life-changing scientist/inventor/mystic.

So the next time you feel yourself breaking away from the herd, throwing off the burden of the mundane, mediocre, and unimaginative norm, congratulate yourself. You are now in the company of true greatness!

Emanuel Swedenborg
and Dream Work

*I*n addition to being fascinating and fun, dream work can be a great way to engage in the classic "know thyself" quest. However the value in dream work does not stop there. Dreams can be a profound way to grow and evolve Spiritually as well. Throughout history, and even before recorded history, dreams have been regarded as a portal into the Spiritual Realm. What most dream workers do not know is the amazing documented dream work of Emanuel Swedenborg.

Long before Freud coined the words "conscious" and "unconscious", Swedenborg was recording his dreams in what would become one of the largest collections of dream journals ever amassed. In addition to recording his *Journal of Dreams* for twenty-six years, he also wrote a five-volume *Spiritual Diary*. Swedenborg examined the nature of dream reality and its relationship to mind and Spirituality, one hundred years before Carl Jung. Jung, by the way, was greatly influenced by Swedenborg.

Swedenborg had some very interesting things to say about dreams and dreaming. He says that when we dream, we are doing more than merely rehashing the day's events. Swedenborg states that if you wanted to pick up the phone and hear what the Divine has to say about your life, you will pay attention to your dreams. Dreaming is when higher order beings (Angels, spirit guides, etc.) come and speak to us in a symbol language that is constantly commenting on the quality of our love. Dreaming is a time when we reconnect with the Divine; we all need this alignment, which is why our minds start to unravel if we are deprived of REM time reconnection.

Swedenborg says the Pharaoh's dreams that Joseph interpreted, the dreams of King Nebuchadnezzar, and those of Biblical prophets are not brought by Angels to an individual, but rather "flow" directly from a higher level of Heaven to the sleeping person. In fact all dreams that are prophetic in nature are communicated this way — directly from Prime Source to the receiver. (It's a Divine Hotline, not to be confused with The Psychic Hotline.) Swedenborg compared dreaming to "Divine Visions" saying that dreams of this type are "Divine Visions" experienced during a sleeping state of mind, rather than a waking state of mind. I can only imagine that most people would be more open to receiving the content of a "Divine Vision" in a dreaming state, because our perception of waking reality is so rigid, most people would think they were losing their mind or grip on reality, if the "Divine Vision" visited them during normal business hours.

Swedenborg says that while he was exploring the Spiritual Realm, he learned about dreams and dreaming from the other side. He says that he was able to learn from direct experience what dreams are and how they are communicated. Swedenborg writes that he was learning directly from the Angels who introduced the dreams to the dreamer. He closely observed this process of dream introduction from Angel to dreaming human. He also says he was given the opportunity to learn by assuming the role of the Angel, and being the agent who actually introduced a pleasant dream to another. Through this hands-on participation in these experiences, he gained comprehensive and very exclusive knowledge. His groundbreaking dream work and research is absolutely remarkable and transcends any understanding or theory about the origin, nature, function or purpose of dreams ever gathered, either before or after Swedenborg's lifetime.

As a matter of fact Swedenborg says that his initiation into his life as a mystic started with his dreams in dream time. Swedenborg's journal shows that he started having a series of dreams that were sometimes very disturbing in nature. These dreams offered him a commentary on his intellectual and scientific affections. Swedenborg said he realized eventually that all the scientific work he had been doing was a huge burden, similar to carting a load of heavy rocks around with him everywhere he went. When Swedenborg began his life as a mystic, working on mapping out the Spiritual World and explaining its method and nature of operation, he completely gave up his life as a scientist. He devoted the remainder of his life to his Spiritual investigations, for which all of us, who have come after Swedenborg, are eternally grateful and wiser.

What has most impressed me about Swedenborg's wisdom about dreams is that they are all about love! Dreams ask us to examine honestly and fearlessly what we are doing with our love — our attention. Oftentimes dreams are protecting and healing us with the quality of their Divine wholeness-making love. It's no wonder so many of us are compelled to know about our dreams and to explore dream time ceaselessly. We are driven by our love to know and understand more about the infinite nature of Divine Love and Wisdom, and quite frankly, I cannot imagine a better use of our time while here visiting the planet Earth. So, in response to that, may I say, that I know that flights of Angels *will* sing thee to thy rest. And remember, for the ultimate in "wake-up calls", there is always the canon of Divinely guided wisdom left to us by the remarkable Emanuel Swedenborg. Sweet dreams!

You Haven't Lived Until You've Died

We call it *"the afterlife"*. But from everything we know about it, we really should be calling it *"the life"*, and calling what we are experiencing now *"the before life"*. There has been so much documented and recorded about what happens after we die, that its mere existence is indisputable. If you are a die-hard westerner in your thought process, there are the books by Dr. Brian Weiss like *Many Masters, Many Lives*, and Dr. Michael Newton's, *Life Between Lives*. For those who are more adventuresome of Spirit there is *Ordered to Return: My Life After Dying* by George G. Ritchie, Jr. M.D., and Dannion Brinkley's *Saved By The Light*. But the greatest wisdom, the glittering diamond of transcendent knowledge, has to be the writings of Emanuel Swedenborg. He is the quintessential one-stop shopping for "afterlife" wisdom.

If you are looking for an expert on the "afterlife", Swedenborg is a pretty tough act to follow. So enough of this post-human foreplay . . . just what does Swedenborg have to say about the other side of the veil? A few things, depending on your background, might surprise you. Swedenborg says that when we cross over we still have our senses; we still appear to have a body not unlike our Earthly counterpart, except the Spiritual version is minus any pain, illness, old age or cellulite. Actually, I just made up that last part. He never mentioned cellulite. But a girl can dream, can't she? Swedenborg says we still see, hear, feel and look much the way we did in physical life, so that our transition from protoplasm to ethereal is a kinder, gentler experience. The next thing that may surprise you is that Swedenborg says there is no judgment day - like that one you were most likely terrorized with in Sunday school. As a matter of fact, according to Swedenborg, God is incapable of judging us or getting mad at us. God is only capable of unconditional love, acceptance, tolerance and forgiveness. That is the good news. Now for the bad news: we judge ourselves. That's right. The only judgment going on in the afterlife is the judgment we bring upon ourselves. This is the primary reason Swedenborg suggests we practice letting go of judgment here while we can. When we take it with us to the other side, it becomes a much more difficult attachment to break.

Not only are we the only ones that judge us, but Swedenborg also says we all go directly the highest level of Heaven, regardless of how we may have lived our lives on Earth. But as Shakespeare might have said it, "Here is the rub." We do not all stay in the most liberated level of Heaven. Why, you might ask? Good question. And the answer is equally as compelling: not because someone kicks us out or tells us we have to leave, but because *we* are not comfortable staying there! That's right. We evict our own ethereal butts!

If you have spent your entire life telling yourself that you are not deserving and worthy of love and happiness, you will slide right out of Celestial Heaven like a slinky working its way down Jacob's ladder, until you find your most comfortable level. If your whole life centered around "looking out for number one," well guess what numero uno? You might exit the highest level of Heaven running and screaming like a little girl, because the citizens of Heaven all take care of each other and look out for each other equally. Remember, he who dies with the most toys is still dead. There is no #1 in Heaven . . . other than everyone!

Maybe you have spent your whole life looking over your shoulder, just waiting for someone to hurt, scam or otherwise abuse you. You are not going to be spending much time in upper-level paradise either, because no one there is comfortable living that way. The citizens of Heaven have all given up that habit for embracing, supporting and trusting one another. I wonder just how many of us will be comfortable living in a world we all say we want, but do not practice creating or living in while here on Earth?

What I found most interesting about Swedenborg's descriptions of the afterlife is that once on the other side, everyone knows the truth. Oh, don't get me wrong; it is not like everyone in the next realm always *tells* the truth. Prevarication apparently happens everywhere. But on the other side, when someone speaks a "terminological inexactitude", their voice becomes harsh and grating. It is like a large beacon going off over their head saying, "I'm lying, I'm lying." I don't know about you, but as far as I'm concerned, that is worth dying for.

"If there is no God, who pops up the Kleenex?"

A Mystic Perspective on
Aliens or E.S. Phone Home

*W*e all know that scientists around the world have been searching for alien life. They have been behaving like the ultimate in universal voyeurs, keeping a roving eye out for signs of "other worldly life forms", poised listening, like the nosey eavesdropping neighbor, for any possible alien transmissions — intergalactic messages. We are also familiar with the various scenarios science fiction writers have depicted as possible outcomes of alien and human life reaching out and touching one another. It runs from "Star Trek" to "The Martian Chronicles" and Spielberg's "E.T." to "Independence Day", "Mars Attacks" and even "I Had An Alien's Baby" in the supermarket tabloids. At least the science fiction writers are more creative and broad-minded in their speculative surmising. Between the hard measurable facts and the flights of human imaginative fancy *is* there some information that exists, right now, about the actuality of alien life, and how they may be responding to us? The answer is ... yes! The source however may surprise you. The author I will be drawing upon has impeccable credentials and has attained an unquestionable level of scientific and academic accomplishment. His observations, however, may read to many like the ramblings of an over-inventive, over-active imagination. Sound interesting? Well, it is! And, this author's books and writings about his contact with alien life forms have been around for hundreds of years and published in dozens of languages. Stumped? Allow me the pleasure of introducing Emanuel Swedenborg to you.

257

Emanuel Swedenborg left his scientific ventures behind when he discovered something infinitely more compelling . . . Spiritual exploration. He wrote over a million words on the nature of nonphysical existence and the life forms that inhabit it.

Among his many exhaustive literary efforts is a very slim book that has just been reprinted and re-released called *Life On Other Planets,* with a forward by Dr. Raymond Moody, a rational man of science and logic. In this book, Emanuel Swedenborg talks about his non-ordinary reality visits to many planets, including some outside our solar system. When I use the term "non-ordinary reality" my intention is to use it in the same context as a shaman or remote viewer might "visit" another place without the limitations and restrictions of the human body. In this book, Emanuel Swedenborg first travels to Mercury, where he proceeds to cite his observations with the discipline and focus of a refined man of science. What he documents in his space trekking is what should be our most significant concern in this matter of alien life: what these aliens value, what is important to them, how and if they might contact us.

The question of how will aliens respond according to what they value gets astoundingly myopic consideration. Saturday Night Live considered these same questions with not so surprisingly different results. One of our U.S. space probes contained samples of all Earth languages along with music from Mozart to Chuck Berry. According to the SNL news reporting team, "NASA has received an alien transmission . . . it contains only three words . . . 'more Chuck Berry'." Aside from Swedenborg, that is the most honest consideration of their needs recorded to date.

Swedenborg says that all the life forms he visited in this solar system and beyond were humanoid in appearance, but they are not having a carbon based physical experience in a three dimensional world in the way that we are. They have social and family structures, and they are all well aware of the reality that there is only one God. Moreover they know that they will live on after their present "bodies" perish. They also seem to be aware of us as well, and our . . . well, how shall I put it . . . lack of Spiritual breeding. It would seem that to other alien life forms, we are perceived as the banjo picking, toothless, inbred hillbillies of the Universe. When Swedenborg first traveled to the planet Mercury, the beings there were unwilling to communicate with him. The Spirits of Mercury openly expressed their disdain at having to interact with a race of beings so far beneath them, since we do not even know there is only one God, and we think that when one dies that is it. From their point of view, that puts us near the bottom of the list when it comes to intelligent life forms.

The Spirits of Mercury as Swedenborg describes them worship the gathering and accumulation of facts. They have a great capacity for storing and retaining information. They are not fettered by a physical existence and henceforth travel the Universe in search of expanding their collection and cannon of knowledge. They are extremely unimpressed by anything of a physical origin. They abhor it so much they do not talk, because speech is too contaminated by a physical process. They prefer instead to engage in what Swedenborg called "thought activation." In *Life On Other Planets* Swedenborg sums up what these Spirits value: ". . . the Spirits of Mercury are not particularly distinguished for their powers of judgment. They take no pleasure in matters requiring judgment or in inferences from known facts. It is the bare facts that give them pleasure." When Swedenborg tried to show the Spirits of Mercury things on Earth like rivers, lakes, oceans, or castles, they blotted it out claiming things of a physical nature hold no value to them. It would seem NASA would not fare well with the Spirits of Mercury, as NASA has no bare facts outside of the physical realm to offer their neighbor nearest the Sun. (Obviously these Spirits did not send NASA the Chuck Berry message. They are more like the Sergeant Joe Friday of the Solar System, "Just the facts ma'am; just the facts.").

On to Saturn, where Swedenborg describes these aliens as very humble and focused on Divine Love and Wisdom. He says that they frequently speak with other Spiritual beings, which we would call alien life forms. However when the conversation strays from the worship of Prime Source, they lose attention and return their focus to the one God. Swedenborg says their devotion is so intensely committed to this alignment with God, that they would rather die than change. Again, NASA, with their scientific agenda, is going to have a difficult time enticing contact with these planetary neighbors. So far the score is Aliens 2, NASA 0.

Moving on to Jupiter, Swedenborg says that after an inhabitant of that planet dies, they continue to interact with the aliens there and to be of service as a Spirit. I know some could argue that happens here as well, but I do not think that is a reality NASA is ever going to recognize, at least not publicly. The aliens of Jupiter, as Swedenborg describes them, are very sweet, loving beings. They value their children foremost. They do not want, desire or steal what they do not already possess. When Swedenborg tried to share the social makeup of our world, the natives of Jupiter found it so offensive, they turned their backs and would not listen. Again, I suspect our government would not get far with these aliens, as according to Swedenborg, they DO NOT LIE!

Interestingly enough, Swedenborg notes about the inhabitants of Jupiter that, "They neither know nor wish to know anything about the sciences we have in our world. They call these 'shadows' and liken them to the clouds which obscure the sun."

Swedenborg says that every planet and every moon has a Spiritual life form on it. He says the reason for that is the Universe is the seminar of Heaven. Every planet and moon is a place of learning and growth for the entire Spiritual community at large. Swedenborg describes Divine Love and Wisdom as being the highest, most powerful and most efficient intelligence in the Universe. He assures us that everything Divine Love and Wisdom creates is needed and ultimately useful. So if there was no purpose in creating a huge Universe filled with Solar Systems, Quasars, Black Holes and clusters of Galaxies, it simply would not exist. Furthermore, most everyone else not indigenous to this planet already seems to know that.

If what Swedenborg offers us is indeed a preview of coming attractions, NASA would be better off sending sutras, malas, pujas, prayers and other spiritually related offerings of devotion to our neighbors. At this rate, no one but Earthlings will be at NASA's party. The aliens will undoubtedly have moved on to something infinitely more meaningful, while we sit around and contemplate our vast scientific superiority, that no one else in the Universe could give a comet out-gassing about. Happy space trucking!

Eternal Voices, Infinite Truth

One of the things that has always amazed me, as a seeker of timeless wisdom, is how different people, separated by time and geographic distance, so frequently express the same eternal truths. Case in point the great Swedish mystic Emanuel Swedenborg (1688-1772) born in Stockholm, Sweden and Edgar Cayce (1877-1945) born in Hopkinsville, Kentucky. Both men are regarded, not only as famous seekers of Spiritual wisdom, but also as remarkably gifted in their ability to gain insight and knowledge from the Spiritual realm.

Swedenborg started out his life as a great scientist, looking to master every known science, for one expressed purpose: to find out where the Soul resided in the human experience. He was able to control his breath and, through a tremendous focus of concentration, enter into a trace-like state. Once in that "other worldly" state of consciousness Swedenborg was able to converse with what he described as higher and lower order beings in the purely Spiritual world. He went on to write over 35 volumes of work describing how the Spiritual realm operates, what happens when you die, what Heaven and hell look like, and whatever information on the spiritual world he was given permission to pass on to this physical realm.

Many people came to Swedenborg while he was alive, asking him to use his abilities to acquire information for them. Most of the time people requested that Swedenborg find a deceased loved one to secure information that, for obvious reasons, they could not access themselves.

Edgar Cayce, on the other hand, was a very simple man. With only an eighth grade education, he spent most of his life struggling to find life-sustaining employment and sufficient monetary resources. Cayce suffered with health issues early in his life. He found relief working with a hypnotist, who, after hypnotizing Cayce, asked him to tell the practitioner what the source of his ailment was and how to cure it. Under hypnosis Cayce conveyed the problem, and then proceeded to resolve it in his physical body.

Cayce has sometimes been called the "sleeping prophet" because when he would go into a trance-like state for the information people sought, he was only aware of his own private dreams, not remembering any of the information that came through him. Cayce would lay down, go under, and all his communication would be recorded by his wife or personal secretary. Conversely, Swedenborg remained fully aware of his contact with the other side, as well as being aware of what was happening on the physical side of reality simultaneously.

What these two extraordinarily phenomenal men do have in common is that both men would "check in" with the other side to see if the information being asked of them was beneficial to bring back and share with others. If they felt they were being instructed to drop the request, then the person asking would leave empty handed. Both men operated out of a state of great untarnished integrity in this matter. No amount of pressure or bribery could influence them to retrieve information they felt they had been advised not to procure. These men, like Hebrew National, knew they had to answer to a "higher authority".

Another thing both these men had in common was their understanding about the nature of free will. Both men felt very strongly that the power of free will was to be respected and honored in every person's life, as their birthright from the Divine. The coercion of another's free will was a big Spiritual "no no". They also advocated for the human experience being about exploring right relationship with free will:

- that the reason we are all here is to learn how to be in right relationship with what we freely do with our will, love, service and life purpose.

- that free will is such a profound force, it has life as well as earth- changing abilities.

In other words, if a person chooses to align his free will with love, kindness and good faith, then not only would that person's immediate life change, but in changing themselves, they would make the earth a better, more vital place for others as well!

These two men dedicated their entire lives to learning and sharing the highest, most Divinely guided information their exceptional skills and talents could glean. It would seem that in addition to living exemplary lives of honesty and integrity, these men would like us to receive the gift and empowerment that is our birthright as Divinely created beings: claiming the relationship with our free will we were designed to have. It certainly deserves as much, if not more attention than what we regularly give, without reservation, to CNN, the Home Shopping Network and Entertainment Tonight.

Who Are You?

*I*t was the early 1980's, and for weeks I had been looking forward to the *Who* concert at the Astrodome. I was a collector of vintage clothing at the time, and after some consideration, I finally decided to wear a lovely blouse I had recently purchased. It was very distinctive, with an intricate cutout pattern. It would go nicely with my favorite pair of jeans and knee high lace up moccasins.

This concert was shortly after the fatal *Who* concert where several young people had been trampled to death by an out of control crowd. I thought about that briefly, then lovingly admired my "general admission" ticket - my passport to an evening with Pete Townshend and Roger Daltry. I knew this would place me on the floor of the Astrodome amidst the thronging masses of other *Who* fans who would no doubt surge forward, like a stampeding herd of wildly driven buffalo, but I decided if I was going to die, at least I was going to go out in a rock and roll blaze of glory.

Shortly before the show, however, I could not shake the feeling that I might find myself packed in next to a drunken teenager, who would spend the evening puking his under-aged brains out, and ruin my lovely vintage top. So, to my date's annoyance, I decided at the last minute to change my outfit. I exchanged the vintage apparel for a brightly colored bowling shirt, proudly displaying a rainbow trout on the back. If nothing else, should my date and I get separated, at least he would have no trouble spotting me in a crowd with this highly visible beacon of a shirt.

Naturally we went as early as possible to begin the impossible task of forging out a spot as close to the stage as possible. The crowd gathered and quickly grew around us. As fate would have it, I found myself jammed tightly next to a highly inebriated adolescent, who spent the last half hour before the lights went out spewing forth a virtual ocean of regenerated alcohol. I managed miraculously to narrowly escape getting soiled throughout the thirty-minute purging episode.

Finally the moment we had all been waiting for - the lights went down, and the excitement level rose as the predictable surge from those behind us pushed us closer to the stage with the power of an incoming wave. Pete was wearing his utilitarian rocker jumpsuit, arms wind milling around in his signature style. Roger was in fine form, his golden locks accentuating his rock star persona. John Entwistle, with his trademark mustache and formidable stature, played the bass guitar with fury.

About an hour into the concert, the inevitable occurred. I had to go to the bathroom. I put off forsaking my hard earned full frontal stage position as long as possible, but when nature calls, even the *Who* cannot stifle its scream. We slowly made our way through the crowd to the back of the Astrodome floor where the people had been divided into an in-going line and an out-going line of human traffic. After waiting for what seemed like an eternity, I finally relieved my bodily fluid burden and was ready to take on the arduous task of returning to the general admission crowd and attempting to forge out a vantage point amidst the sea of frenzied *Who* fans.

As I was standing in line with my date, slowly following the line of people making their way through the in-going traffic lane, I glanced over to the line of people funneling their way through the out-going line, when I caught a glimpse of myself. At first I thought nothing about it. My mind justified the event with the thought that there must be mirrors around. Then the clarity of the situation completely possessed my mind, and I realized that I was on the floor of the Astrodome! They have tractor pulls down here; there are no mirrors anywhere! I looked back to see the image of "myself" partaking in the slow double take as well. On closer examination, I realized that the "me" I was looking at was wearing the coveted vintage blouse I had decided to change at the last minute. I had recently just permed my hair, and the "me" I was looking at had not. We both slowly raised our left hands and pointed at each other, mouths gapping open in total shock and surprise. The soundtrack of the *Who* playing the prophetic song, *Who Are You?* was filling the electrically charged the air. As I was staring at myself, mind you not someone who looked like me, but another parallel version of myself, I could hear Roger Daltry in the background asking, "Who are you . . . I really want to know!" Needless to say it was one of those rare immortal moments in life that defy explanation or rational logic. I was standing, pointing to myself, or at the very least a simultaneous version of myself, with Roger Daltry vocalizing my innermost emotional truth, when I had the thought, "Say something to her!" when I heard myself answer, in my own head, in my own voice . . . "You *are* talking to her! You *are* her!" A sudden calming peace washed over me, as unexplainable as the experience itself. I became aware in that moment that my date, not sharing the same reality as myself, had continued on, and we had become separated by the charge of impatient people pushing their way back on to the concert floor area. I managed to call his name out, and he turned around and made his way back to where I stood, still frozen in place by the mesmerizing power of my doppelgänger.

"I . . . I saw myself! And I recognized myself" I helplessly stammered out. (Try explaining this one to your date!) I retold my tale of non-ordinary reality self-confrontation. Whether he believed me or not I will never know. Maybe he just wanted to get back to music. He responded with a matter of fact attitude that implied that this type of thing happens all the time. "Of course you recognized yourself; you know who you are", he replied while grabbing my hand and moving me back into the flow of traffic. I glanced over my shoulder just in time to see the "other" me disappear into the crowd.

It has been over twenty years since that night in Houston at the Astrodome. The vintage blouse, the bowling shirt and the date have all long ago fallen to the wayside. But the memory of literally running into myself, like the haunting refrain of *"Who are you? I really want to know!"* lingers on. To this day I am no closer to understanding what created that event in time and space. To tell the truth, I have stopped trying. At this point in my life all I can say is . . . ***rock on!***

Epilogue: By Permission of Awareness Magazine

www.awarenessmag.com

You Are What You Love

By Donna Strong

*V*aishāli is a spiritual galvanizing rod, crackling with cutting-edge candor and laser-like clarity. Her first book, *You Are What You Love*, is a tour de force of wit and wisdom. Her writing transcends the confines of regular language, offering mind-bending new perspectives to bring deeper understanding.

As a woman who has undertaken a lengthy study of the great spiritual traditions, she has digested an encyclopedia of esoteric information, offering it with Zen directness and simplicity. In bringing forth the work of Emmanuel Swedenborg, a Swedish mystic and scientist who lived three centuries earlier, she has offered us a font of timeless insight.

It proves its merit by simultaneously addressing the current collective interest in the Law of Attraction. She offers Swedenborg's perspective: You are what you love and you create it in abundance through what you give your attention to. This book makes it pointedly clear; we choose Heaven or hell each moment, based on where we place our attention.

As a street-smart 'doctor of divinity,' Vaishāli's prescription for transforming the ego-ridden ills of present-day life is to offer generous portions of soul food, insightful commentary on what truly sustains our lives, spiced with pithy humor that is right at home. Vaishāli's work certainly affirms the psychology research that wit is a lively form of intelligence.

They say the masters have a great sense of humor, and Vaishāli stands among them, to remind us all that we are able to transcend temporal turbulence as the enduring and eternal flame of awareness that we each are. As a living example of one who has faced great trials as her own life unraveled, the 'V' in her name must surely stand for victory, for she has triumphed in realizing brilliant awareness beyond the muck of the unenlightened mind.

As a diva who pays daily homage to the color purple, she is a shining example of the gifts of the Violet Ray for our age; the ability to transmute and move forward, laughing and free. Unabashedly direct, she has a lightning form of brilliance to not only illuminate ancient wisdom, but also make it crisply modern and sagely savvy.

As we kick off the New Year, we present Vaishāli, a woman who presents her spiritual acumen with a strong dash of verve and vivid color.

Awareness: To begin, please tell us how you came to love the color purple…

Vaishāli: Ever since I was a small child, this color has just fascinated me. I'll tell you an interesting story that might explain it. When I was first putting together, You Are What You Love, I thought I should seek out somebody in the industry who would just give me the straight dope on whether this was something I should pursue, or maybe I shouldn't quit my day job. So I got hold of Dannion Brinkley, and we sent him a copy of the book. After he read it, he said, "This is going to be very, very big."

For the first year after we made contact, we only talked on the phone, so he never saw that everything in my life is purple. I tell people that I had my white and grey matter converted to purple so it wouldn't clash with my accessories. We were talking on the phone one day and he says, "When I look at you energetically, you don't even exist." He said, "Are you familiar with the Violet Flame group?" I said, Yes I am, of course. "When I look at you energetically, this group simply downloads through you, you don't even really exist! You are purely their conduit, and I have never seen that before." So I suspect that explains why since I was a small child, this color has absolutely mesmerized me.

Awareness: I asked you that because I thought there might be a relationship; the Violet Flame is such a potent energy.

Vaishāli: I have a little blurb about it in the book, indicating that it is Shiva's favorite color. Shiva is considered the most powerful of all the Hindu gods, because he was willing to drink the world's poison and transform it into unconditional love. I see the color purple as symbolic of an application of your free will to take the lowest, the world's poison, and to transform it into unconditional love.

Awareness: For me this gets to the core of something I feel is the truth about you so I really appreciate your openness in sharing it. It also illuminates for us that there is something intelligent in our inherent draw to certain colors and interest in subjects we should trust. Can you tell me a bit about how Emmanuel Swedenborg came into your life, since he is such a major figure offering spiritual direction in your compelling book?

Vaishāli: Someone gave me a cassette tape, called The Secrets of the Masters, done by Michael Coleman, who was head professor of Philosophy at Sonoma University at the time. There were many things I recognized in the collection, like existentialism, Freud, and reincarnation, but there was one tape marked Swedenborg, and I had never heard of him.

At that time, I was in my mid-twenties and I had been diagnosed as terminally ill. His whole idea of 'you are what you love' and 'you love whatever you give your attention to,' was the seed that created this vast inner revolution in my life. You know when the Beatles say; 'You want a revolution, you had better free your mind instead.'

I would heartily agree with that. It allowed me to see how the way I was living affected my health. When I really examined this law, 'you are what you love,' and 'you love whatever you give your attention to,' I realized I loved some really limited, non-life sustaining things. There was a direct correlation to what I was fixated on, and how my body was responding. Before being diagnosed as terminal, I had abdominal pain for a year. After having exploratory surgery, my doctor told me all my organs were in crisis. While taking a quarter from his pocket he remarked, "Your liver and small intestines are the worst. I could flip this quarter as to which organ will shut down first."

Because of the difficulties in my life, I had given worry the bulk of my attention. Worry was my drug of choice. It was the first thing I would focus on when I got up in the morning and the last thing I thought about before going to sleep at night. I mainlined worry. My love of it only brought more worry into my life.

When I realized this, I was already in so much pain all the time, I figured what do I have to lose? Swedenborg stated very simply, there is nothing in it for you when you give your attention to anything limiting. So I thought okay, there is nothing I have to lose, my life is already swirling down the drain, so why don't I practice not giving my attention to anything limiting?

I began practicing. When my attention floated back to things that were limiting, I would let them be an inner alarm clock that would awaken me to, "Oh yea, this is not what I want to do with my love!" I didn't spiritually travel from wherever I was to find my goofy butt in a bag of protoplasm.

That is not what I want to do with my love, so I started practicing giving my free will only to what lived in an unlimited place and it created an absolute inner and outer revolution in my life! The more I pulled my butt out of the fire and gained momentum and mastery of this practice, I realized this is something the rest of the world really doesn't get.

Awareness: It is absolutely true. There are qualities of these principles that are well known, but you are a catalyst to wake people up. Love is a powerful force. Yet we try to put it in a little box and keep it 'well-managed' in our lives.

Vaishāli: And it is not! Our palpable living relationship with it is so superficial; it is a short shoddy affair. We think of love in this very limited way, as to do only with things we like or family or pictures that have to do with puppies and kittens. It does not reach the depth of 'You do not have love, you are love.' It is inseparable from your spiritual identity. It is what you brought with you when you came, it is the vehicle by which you experience this planet and it is what you are going to take with you when you leave.

Awareness: One of the things you touched on right there, and your book brilliantly exposes, is how we language everything like it is some kind of property. We are constantly reviewing all of the things that we 'have.'

Vaishāli: The most crucial perception of our spiritual identity, our alignment with love, our value, our power and worth, is that we have it completely at the mercy of the temporal world, so we see it as conditional. Especially with the Puritan work ethic in America, we see it as something that has to be earned or deserved. It needs to be claimed in the eternal category.

Regardless of whether we have gone through a big nasty divorce or people say, "I don't like you because you have a big butt," "You don't have love, you are it." No one or no thing on this planet has the power to change that! Whether you can pay your bills or not, get fired from a job, or whether you have been a housewife your whole life and feel like you don't have value as a workforce commodity, you don't have value, power and worth, you are it! That is eternal and unchanging!

The soul is a sum total of our free will and our love, what we give our attention to, our service, the quality of our relationships and our life purpose. When we move the soul out of the temporal, it allows us to have experiences that we have come to earth to have, and not have our spiritual identity suffer from the experiences we go through. Hopefully our experiences are going to be wide and divergent, because we didn't come here to live in a shoebox.

We need to go from what the temporal world wants to allot us by how well we perform, or how the conditions in the temporal world play themselves out today, all the way across the spectrum to, okay world, throw your best at me. Put me through the sausage factory, do your name calling, after all, this is life on planet earth, but you are not going to change the fact that I don't have value and worth, I am it.

You are still not going to change that I don't have love; I am divine love in this moment. So go ahead and throw your best at me. Everything you throw at me tempers the truth in my mind to a state of absolute perfect unconditionality.

Awareness: Your comments remind me of what it was like as I let go of being a married middle-class woman, and the confines of 'this is as good as it gets in life.' Exploring in the years afterward was alternately painful and expansive; yet there was an inner guidance that kept urging me on to find a place of more freedom, one that felt right.

Vaishāli: We all need to take our lives out of the temporal shoebox and move them to the eternal category, understanding everything that comes isn't coming to diminish you or to make your life more complicated, it comes to serve you and bring an immortal relationship with divine unconditional love that is beyond the annihilation of anything in this world.

Awareness: On a related subject, what can people do in the moment to clear the samskaras {also spelled sanskaras, a word indicating impressions} mentioned in your book? Related to this, you make the fabulous statement, "We're here to practice self soul surgery through self witnessing." Can you tell our readers about how to make this perceptual shift?

Vaishāli: I love the saying; 'the truth shall set you free.' You know, the value of self-witnessing is that when you give your attention to the truth, that is where this tempering comes from that roasts the seeds of karma. No incomplete action comes from it. The idea is, when I give my attention to the truth, that as divine love, it means I do not have God consciousness, I am God consciousness.

As God consciousness, I cannot create a learning experience I don't need. This is how Emmanuel Swedenborg says it. No one on this planet can create a learning experience that we don't need. Only what we need to reach enlightenment is ever allowed to touch our lives.

The example I often give is this: What about the situation where some people get cancer and others don't? What is that about? The people who got cancer needed that experience for the evolution of their souls and the people who didn't get cancer didn't. Only what you need, when you need it, according to Swedenborg in his observations on the power of divine love and wisdom. Everything that happens in your life is working for you or it would not be allowed near your life. Everything, without exception, is working for you.

As Buddhism says, pain is a part of life. Suffering is optional. When you go through life and you experience divorce and illness and monetary challenges, you experience the myriad of different crises that are part and parcel with this packaging.

When you give your attention to 'why is this happening to me,' the level of suffering escalates. The firestorm whips up around you, creating more samskaras, more marks or more impressions of woundedness, of 'I have no power, I have no worth, why was I singled out for this terrible thing to happen to me?'

When you witness a human experience through the flame of truth, that this is serving me or it would not be allowed to show up, it is actually accelerating the evolution of your soul and the liberation of your mind.

Divine love and wisdom is extremely efficient.

It is incapable of manifesting something it does not need. Therefore, rather than coming to this with the firestorm question that only ravages my mind with 'why me,' I am going to come to this and ask the question, 'okay, what's in it for me?'

Only what serves and brings me to enlightenment is allowed to come into my life, to be experienced in my human incarnation. The flame of truth purifies the illusion and destroys the limitation, removing the samskara from your mind.

Awareness: I had an experience of this recently, and it is potently true!

Vaishāli: You know, the truth does set you free. So when you are in the firestorm, stop and witness what you are doing with your attention. If it is not setting you free, it is your spiritual identity's wisdom telling you that you have not seen the truth of it, keep looking.

Awareness: Personally, I have found that when the firestorm is ravaging, I eventually get to the point where I am just willing to let go, because it is so painful and heavy, I am not willing to carry it any more. Would you like to speak to the quality of surrender that you have addressed in your book?

Vaishāli: The first thing that I want to acknowledge is your strongest urge to surrender and let it go is the benefit of spiritual maturity.

Most people would draw it closer to themselves, by virtue of how they define themselves by it.

I am the person this terrible thing happened to; I am the person who got this divorce, whatever the litany. So they draw it closer, and their instinctual response is not to let go and let God, or to allow whatever the evolutionary force is to create an opening and do some spiritual sculpting so their true divine form can emerge. So let me just acknowledge that what you just shared is truly revealing of what you love.

It is our work right now to create that hundredth-monkey infectious response, so that it does become natural to 'let go and let God,' and not simply sleepwalk. When you sleepwalk through life, you don't realize how much energy you give away to things that will take you emotionally, psychologically and spiritually to a limited existence.

When you ask most people if they want to have vibrant health, abundant finances, and quality healthy relationships, they would say "Yes, sign me up," but when you say the price is being aware of what you give your attention to, suddenly nobody is interested.

Awareness: Yes, there is still a big disconnect.

Vaishāli: There is a big disconnect. Surrender is a free-fall of 'I can't create a learning experience I don't need, therefore whatever force is moving through my life right now is creating a spiritual revolution, an evolutionary advance, and I will allow the gift of divine love and wisdom to shape and mold and create the perfect vessel.'

Intellectually you are trying to figure out how to get out of situations that are painful or how you can change the situation more toward your ego's agenda and how it defines the experience. What is happening is infinitely greater than the ego's opinion.

Surrender is a non-intellectualized state that is the wisdom of a heart aligned with the truth; the awareness that I don't have love, I am love.

For more information about Vaishāli her books, radio show and other events, please visit:www.youarewhatyoulove.com or www.purplehazepress.com

Donna Strong's first book, Coming Home to Calm, will be published in January 2008. She can be reached at www.donnastrong.com.

Published in Awareness Magazine, January/February 2007, www.awarenessmag.com

Other Books By
Purple Haze Press:

You Are What You Love
By Vaishāli
You Are What You Love is the definitive 21st century guide for Spiritual seekers of timeless wisdom who have hit a pothole on the way to enlightenment and are searching for the answers to the big questions in life: "Who am I?" and "Why am I here?" Author Vaishāli explores mystic Emanuel Swedenborg's philosophy of gratitude and love. She expands this wisdom by associating it to traditional sources including Christianity and Buddhism. Through storytelling and humor, the focal point of the book "you don't have love, you are love" is revealed. A compelling read to deepen your understanding of Oneness.

Paperback, 400 pages, ISBN 978-0-9773200-0-4, $24.95

Also available on CD an 80-minute condensed and abridged version of the 400-page book counter part. Read by the author.

CD, ISBN 978-0-9773200-2-8, $14.95

You Are What You Love Playbook
By Vaishāli

You Are What You Love Playbook is a playtime manual offering practical play practices to invoke play into action. Included is step-by-step guidance on dream work, a 13-month course in how to practice playful miracles, and a copy of the author's lucid dream diary. The perfect companion to You Are What You Love.

Paperback, 124 pages, ISBN 978-0-9773200-1-1, $14.95

Wisdom Rising
By Vaishāli

Sometimes wisdom is best served up like M&M candies, in small pieces that you can savor, enjoy and hold in your hand. So it is with Vaishāli's new book, "Wisdom Rising." It is a delightful, sweet, and satisfying collection of brilliant articles and short stories, that like gem quality jewels, are a thing of beauty, and a joy to behold.

It doesn't matter what your background is there is something to appeal to everyone in this book. Vaishāli's trademark "out of the box" sense of humor and wild woman perspective runs rampant throughout the book. Whether she is talking about the Nature of God or simply poking fun at our own cultural insecurities and hypocrisies, Vaishāli raises the bar on laugh out loud Spiritual wisdom. The entertainment as well as the wisdom rises flawlessly together, inviting the reader to go deeper in examining and showing up for their own life.

Everything about this book from the cover to the cartoon illustrations that punctuate every story, screams playful, fun, witty, and what we have seen Vaishāli dish up before . . . which is the unexpected . . . no wonder she is know as "the Spiritual Wild Child."

Paperback, ISBN: 978-0-9773200-6-6 $14.95

LONGINUS:
BOOK I OF THE MERLIN FACTOR
by Steven Maines

Longinus follows the tale of Gaius Cassius Longinus, the Roman Centurion who pierced the side Jesus with his spear while the condemned one hung from the cross.

After that fateful day, Longinus escapes Rome and the priests who want to take the spear and its supposed power for themselves. LONGINUS follows the Centurion's life from his love for the prostitute Irena to his mystical studies with the Druids of Gaul. But it also reveals Longinus' profound spiritual awakening through his Druidic studies and the spear that speaks to him with the voice of Christ.

Paperback, 241 pages, ISBN 978-0-9773200-3-5, $14.95

This abridged audio version of the critically acclaimed novel, LONGINUS: BOOK I OF THE MERLIN FACTOR by Steven Maines, follows the tale of Gaius Cassius Longinus, the Roman Centurion who pierced the side of Jesus with his spear while the condemned one hung from the cross. Abridged Audio Book (3 CD). As Read By Mark Colson

CD, ISBN 978-0-9773200-7-3, $19.95

MYRRIDDIN:
BOOK II OF THE MERLIN FACTOR
by Steven Maines

In *MYRRIDDIN: Book II Of The Merlin Factor*, it is the 4th Century A.D. A young boy has found sacred relics of the early Christians in the ruins of an ancient Druid temple on the Isle of Mystery in Old Britain. For reasons beyond his immediate comprehension, the lad connects with one item in particular; the Spear of Longinus, the very spear that pierced the side of Jesus and allegedly holds the power of Christ. The boy's name is Myrriddin. The world would remember him as Merlin, the greatest Druid and Wizard of all time.

Paperback, 217 pages, ISBN 978-0-9773200-4-2, $14.95

Children of the Luminaries
by Julia K. Cole

Do you Believe in the Power of Love?
Imagine everything you held dear was suddenly and viciously destroyed in one night by a power-hungry mad man, and now you find yourself being one of only thirteen survivors of a once mighty and powerful race of people.

Imagine that you have learned of another world, much like your own, with the same impending fate. Imagine being presented "the ultimate power", but not knowing what it is or how to use it. Imagine the realization that the future of a billion souls rests upon your shoulders.

How far would you go to save an entire world not your own? What would you be willing to do? How far would you be willing to go to stop the evil that now plagues a world not your own?

Journey with The Oracle and her mentor Demetrius as they race through time and dimensions to stop the dark lord Dagon and put an end to his maniacal plan to obtain the ultimate power and become ruler of all worlds. Bear witness to the quest and to the incredible transformation of The Oracle herself as she goes from naïve spiritualist to one of the most powerful champions of the Universe.

In the end . . . will Love prevail? Do You Believe?

Paperback, ISBN 978-1-935183-00-6, $19.95

Journey Through the Light and Back
by Mellen-Thomas Benedict

In 1982 Mellen-Thomas died of terminal brain cancer and survived to tell about it. While in hospice care Mellen "died" and was without vital signs for at least an hour and a half before he returned to his body.

While on the "other side" Mellen journeyed through several realms of consciousness and beyond the "Light at the end of the tunnel." He was shown in holographic detail Earth's past and a beautiful vision of mankind's future for the next 400 years. He experienced the cosmology of our soul's connection to Mother Earth (Gaia), our manifest destiny, and was gifted with access to Universal Intelligence.

Paperback, ISBN 978-1-935183-01-3 $19.95

Hitchhiker's Guide to the Other Side
(or what to do if you wake up dead)
by Mellen-Thomas Benedict

Based on his real life experience with terminal illness, loss of all hope and his own death. The story of Mellen-Thomas and his NDE has become one of the world's most popular stories about hope and eternal life.

With love and humor Mellen shares his personal insights on death as an interactive and hopeful experience. This book will enlighten and prepare you for what to expect when you or a loved one leaves this life. This is the first practical guide book to the "Other Side" by someone who has been there and returned.

Paperback, ISBN 978-1-935183-03-7 $14.95